JIM PETRO
AUDITOR OF STATE

STATE OF OHIO

Dear Readers:

As Auditor of State of Ohio, and custodian of state-owned land records, I am proud to introduce the newly designed Ohio Lands book.

The book is a short history of original land treaties, grants, surveys and subdivisions used by teachers, historians, genealogists and others. The new book offers expanded historical analysis through versions written at both the adult and elementary school level.

As part of my official duties, I am responsible for maintaining the inventory and deed records of state-owned real estate.

The office has held this responsibility since 1877, when all of the federal land surveys, field notes, and tract and entry books concerning Ohio were placed in the Auditor's care. All the instruments which show any right, title or interest in state-owned land, except highways, were required to be filed with the Auditor.

All of these records are available either at the Auditor of State's Land Office or at the State Archives.

This book provides a fascinating glimpse into the development of Ohio. As we prepare to celebrate its bicentennial in 2003, I invite readers to delve into the heritage of this great state I am proud to call home.

Best Regards,

Jim Petro

Jim Petro

Auditor of State

Along the Ohio Trail
Table of Contents

Did you know that Ohio is almost the same distance across as it is up and down (about 200 miles)? Our state is shaped in an unusual way. Some people think it looks like a flag waving in the wind. Others say it looks like a heart. The shape is mostly caused by the Ohio River on the east and south and Lake Erie in the north. It is the 35th largest state in the U.S. Can you look at the map of the U.S. on the introduction page and tell which 5 states have boundaries that touch Ohio?

Hi! I'm Simon and I'll be your trail guide as we learn about the land we call Ohio.

Along the Ohio Trail: A Short History of Ohio Lands

Researched and Written by:
Tanya West Dean, B.A., History, Wittenberg University
and W. David Speas, B.S., Education, Heidelberg College

Edited by:
Dr. George W. Knepper, Distinguished Professor of History,
Emeritus, The University of Akron.

This book is a publication of
The Auditor of State
Jim Petro
88 East Broad Street
Columbus, Ohio 43216-1140

www.auditor.state.oh.us
email: petro@auditor.state.oh.us

Third paperback edition 2002

Printed in the United States of America

Introduction

Ohio is the 17th state of the United States of America. We in Ohio think of our state as a "Midwestern" state. People who live on the east coast of the U.S. describe Ohio as a western state, but people who live west of the Mississippi River think of Ohio as an eastern state. Residents of Georgia or Florida say Ohio is a northern state. However, if you lived in Michigan or Wisconsin, Ohio would be south of you.

What does all this mean? Only that Ohio is a lot of different things to different people. Long ago the Iroquois people named the river that forms the southern and eastern boundaries of our state. They called the river a word that sounded like "O-Y-O," meaning "great water." When Europeans heard the word "O-Y-O," they turned it into the word we used today: Ohio. Soon the entire area north and west of the Ohio River was known as Ohio Country.

Our state is an important one in this nation. As you will learn, most of the land areas that became states of the U.S. were patterned after Ohio.

Ohio is considered to be a midwestern state.

Ohio Geography

(state insect) (A)

(state bird) (B)

(state fossil) (C)

(state flower) (D)

(state animal) (E)

(state mineral) (F)

Ohioans have helped form the nation into what it is today. Men and women from Ohio have been great leaders — from Presidents to people who helped slaves gain their freedom, from the first pilots to our nation's greatest astronauts.

Ohio is a beautiful state. It has hills, valleys, farmlands, rivers, lakes, and forests. Each of the four seasons brings about a different beauty in the Ohio lands. Summers are humid and rainy, which causes good growth for both farming and forests. Autumn brings strong harvests and changing leaf colors. Winters are cold, allowing the land to rest in preparation for the coming spring when fields are planted and trees blossom with new leaves. The cycle of growth continues year after year as the land produces the best it has to offer.

Many of the symbols of the state of Ohio come from the land itself. The state nickname, "the Buckeye State," was created because of the plentiful buckeye trees [see graphic (G)] that grow here. The "fruit" on these trees at first has a bumpy surface, but when the outer shell is removed, the nut inside is a deep brown color, with one tan dot. This nut looks like the eye of a deer (or "buck"), so the name "buckeye" was only natural. The leaves on a buckeye tree are made of five leaflets, which look like a hand that is spread out and open. The buckeye became the official state tree in 1953.

Other state symbols that come from the land include:

- **ladybug** (state insect) (A)
- **cardinal** (state bird) (B)
- **trilobite** (state fossil) (C)
- **scarlet carnation** (state flower) (D)
- **deer** (state animal) (E)
- **flint** (state mineral) (F)

Not all of Ohio's symbols come from the land or its natural environment. There are also other symbols of the state of Ohio that are not objects of nature. These important man-made symbols include the State Flag of Ohio and the Great Seal of the State of Ohio.

(buckeye leaf with fruit) (G)

Glaciers and Land Forms

Geologists (people who study the "rock history" of the earth) believe that our planet has gone through several very cold weather periods. They call these periods ice ages. Ohio's last ice age seems to have ended about 12,000 years ago. During an ice age, huge glaciers are formed. Glaciers are large bodies of ice that spread over land and sometimes move slowly down slopes and valleys. As a glacier moves, either by spreading out or by sliding, it also moves some of the earth's materials along with it. Very large glaciers actually can move huge parts of the land's surface, flattening hills and forming valleys and ridges. The bigger the glacier, the more it can change the land over which it moved.

Ohio's last glacier was like that. Geologists believe the glacier was formed in the area we now call Canada. The glacier grew so large that it began to move, eventually covering about two-thirds of Ohio [see graphic (H)]. The thickest part of the glacier might have been about 8,000 feet thick. That's about five times taller than the Sears Tower in Chicago (1,454 feet), one of the U.S.'s tallest buildings. A glacier this large had to weigh millions of tons (and a ton is 2,000 pounds!). When something this big moves, it takes a lot of material with it, pushing the land like a gigantic earthmover [see graphic (I)].

Because of this "earthmover," Ohio's landforms were changed. Some rivers and lakes were filled in with land that moved with the glaciers. Some areas were "carved out." As the glaciers moved, different materials were picked up in the ice. Some of these materials included sand, gravel, soil, and minerals. They were moved from the northern areas

Remains of glacier power can be seen at the Glacial Grooves State Memorial on Kelleys Island in Lake Erie. (I)

Glaciated

Unglaciated

Graphic (H)

page 2

Graphic (J)

because of the deposits left by glaciers. This area, the Till Plains, is a rich farming region. The soil of this region is deep and good for growing crops like corn and soybeans. A large deposit of material can be found in Logan County, which is also the highest point in Ohio. Campbell Hill is 1549 feet above sea level. It is interesting to discover that the lowest point in Ohio is also in the Till Plains region. Only 455 feet above sea level, this low point can be found along the Ohio River near Cincinnati.

The Lake Plains are found in the northwestern part of Ohio and along Lake Erie. These flat plains were formed by glaciers depositing sand and soil near what used to be a much larger lake, Lake Maumee. Because that lake had been larger, some of this area remained swamp

where the glaciers began to various places in the Ohio region. The surface of land was changed as the glaciers moved farther and farther south. These materials were deposited as the glaciers began to melt.

These changes in the surface of Ohio's land caused five different natural regions to be formed [see graphic (J)].

A mix of soil and rock, called till, covers most of the western half of Ohio

Along the Ohio Trail

Of course, I wasn't around when the glaciers were, but I think I can show you how they worked. You could try this experiment (and probably should do it outside). First, freeze some water into a large, flat shape. Then get a board, bigger than the ice, and cover it with pebbles, sand, soil, or any other material. Lay the board at a slight slant. Place the "glacier" at the top of the board. Leave it to melt and move on its own. What happened to the:
- "high" places? What would a glacier do to hills?
- lighter materials?
- heavier materials?
- low areas on the board? What would a glacier do to valleys?
- "land" at the top of the board?
- "land" at the bottom?

After doing this experiment, answer this question: In Ohio, which area would be flatter: the glaciated or unglaciated area?

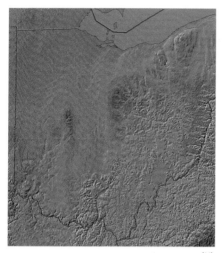

Topographical map of Ohio   *Graphic* (K)

plateau (the northern and western part where the glaciers had been) and the unglaciated plateau (the southern and eastern part where glaciers never reached). The glaciated part has some productive farmland. However, the unglaciated part is so hilly and rugged that farms cannot be developed easily, except in river valleys. It is an area with hardwood trees, rivers, hills, and valleys. Ohio's first settlers lived in this region.

A very small region, known as the Lexington Plain, is also unglaciated. It is in southern Ohio.

for a long time. The Black Swamp area was covered by water much of the time and thick forests grew there. People did not settle in this area until the late 1800s, when the land was drained and used for farming. Then it became some of the most fertile land in Ohio and the United States.

The Allegheny Plateau is actually made up of two regions: the glaciated

Even today, Ohio is shaped by what the glaciers did [see graphic (K)]. The rural (farming) areas of the state lie in the flat regions of the northwest and the hilly regions of the southeast. Diagonally from the southwest corner (near Cincinnati) to the northeast corner (near Cleveland), Ohio has many large cities.

Along the Ohio Trail

The buckeye tree wasn't just an ordinary tree for early settlers. They didn't make their houses out of buckeye wood, but they did make other important things. The wood was very easy to work with. People made chairs, benches, cradles, and even bowls from buckeye wood.

The wood from the buckeye tree was so popular that at one time the species of tree almost vanished from Ohio. Can you think of other items settlers could make from the wood they found in Ohio Country?

Lakes, Rivers, and Forests

When a glacier moved into an area where the ground was soft, it often scooped out some land. Then when the ice melted, it filled the low area with water, making a lake. This can happen on a large or small scale. The Great Lakes, the largest surface fresh water system in the world, were formed this way. Lake Erie has been important in Ohio for transportation, fishing, and recreation. Other smaller lakes in Ohio were also formed by glaciers. There are not many deep lakes in Ohio, and the largest lakes of inland Ohio are all man-made. They were made to handle the extra water that was needed during Ohio's canal era. Now they are mainly used for recreation.

While Ohio is not known for having many lakes, it is known for its great river systems [see graphic (L)]. Streams and rivers run for more than 44,000 miles in this state. Geologists know that Ohio's rivers at one time flowed to the north, but the glaciers blocked them, so the water forced its way along new paths. Flowing water is a powerful force and can cut through land, even bedrock.

The Ohio River is the primary river of Ohio. It forms more than 400 miles of the state's boundary. At one time, it was a major highway heading west, carrying canoes and flatboats for Native Americans, explorers, traders, and settlers.

Ohio's rivers also provide power and resources. Streams and rivers powered the area's mills — and later, factories. Cities and towns grew near the rivers because of this, and because rivers allowed them to travel and trade. Agriculture was strong in river areas. Drinking water was plentiful, both from streams and underground sources, such as springs. Over the years, pollution of Ohio's water has been a problem. Pollution controls have been established to clean up Ohio's lakes, rivers, and underground water sources.

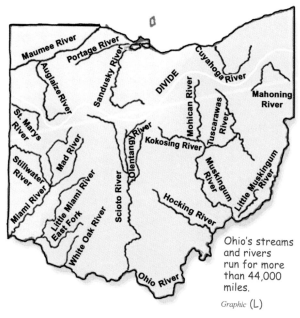

Ohio's streams and rivers run for more than 44,000 miles.

Graphic (L)

Thanks to the rich soil and the ample water supply, forests have grown easily in Ohio. For a long time, the most plentiful raw materials were Ohio's trees, used for timber. Some trees were quite large — their trunks sometimes were as much as seven feet across. Ohio has many different kinds of trees. The most plentiful ones are oak, elm, maple, beech, walnut, and ash trees.

As more settlers and farmers moved into the Ohio Country, many trees were cut down. In order not to lose this important resource, today conservationists have helped to set aside areas just for forests. These lands are protected by the government. Many of

Graphic (M)

The result of natural factors working on parent materials is that Ohio has a great variety of specific soils. This map shows locations of the major soil regions in Ohio

these areas are state parks [see graphic (N)].

This map shows the state parks that are found in Ohio in the year 2000.

Graphic (N)

Raw Materials

A raw material is something found in nature that can be turned into something useful or valuable. Ohio has many raw materials. The primary ones are rock, salt, clay, coal and other minerals.

Useful rock can be found in a quarry, a place where bedrock is found and is cut into shapes used for building. Some of this rock can be crushed and used for other purposes. The main rocks in Ohio are limestone and sandstone. Sand and gravel are plentiful in our state, and these are used in making highways and concrete.

Salt is necessary for humans and animals to live. Early explorers looked for salt as they traveled into new areas. In the Ohio Country, they found a good supply. In fact, Licking County was named for the salt licks found there. A salt lick is a place where salt is deposited (usually by a spring) and animals come to lick it. Salt was used for preserving meat before refrigeration was invented. Today salt is still mined in Ohio, mostly in the northeastern part of the state.

Ohio is a top producer of clay in the United States. It is plentiful in the eastern Allegheny region of the state. Pottery, tiles, pipes, bricks, and other household objects are made of this clay. Some of the largest potteries in the world can be found in Ohio.

Minerals used to be plentiful here, too. Iron ore, coal, petroleum, and natural gas have been important products to our state. In the 1800s, Ohio was one of the most important sources of iron in the world, but after mining it for decades, the iron ore is almost gone. Southern Ohio became developed primarily because of the iron industry. One town in Lawrence County is even named Ironton.

Coal is an important source of energy. It is a black rocklike material that crumbles easily when hit. Much of eastern Ohio has coal, found in layers beneath the ground's surface. Coal is burned, which creates energy. At one time people heated their homes with coal and cooked on coal-burning stoves.

Petroleum (oil) and natural gas are also sources of energy. Today the U.S. imports most of its oil from foreign countries. In the late 1800s, about half of all the oil used in the U.S. came from Ohio. Oil fields were established in Perry, Fairfield, Licking, Allen, Hancock, and other counties. Today oil production continues here in Ohio. Natural gas is also still produced, especially in southeastern Ohio.

Petroleum oil originates in marine waters. It forms as the tiny remains of plants settle in sand and mud. Over a very long period of time the oil accumulates in sand and shale, from which it can be extracted.

Graphic (O)

Prehistoric Ohio

Ohio lands hold many mysteries. Some have been solved by scientists who study prehistoric areas. Some of Ohio's mysteries may never be solved. We do know one thing — Ohio has been a good land for many people for a very long time.

Long before the European explorers traveled into Ohio, people lived here. They are called prehistoric people because they lived before any records about how they lived were written down. When people arrived, who wrote and recorded history, the prehistoric period ended. The cutoff date of the prehistoric period in Ohio is around 1600 A.D. when Europeans began exploring this region.

The oldest evidence of people living in Ohio tells us they were here around 13,000 B.C. Anthropologists, scientists who study ancient people and cultures, have a theory. Many of them believe that Asian people (from China, for example) over a period of many, many years traveled by land from Asia into the present-day state of Alaska. Long ago the two continents of Asia and North America were connected there. However, the last glaciers left behind the waterway we now call the Bering Strait [see graphic (P)], which separates Asia from Alaska. As the people traveled, they moved south and east, migrating into and across Canada, America, Central America, and even into South America. Of course, this took centuries and several generations.

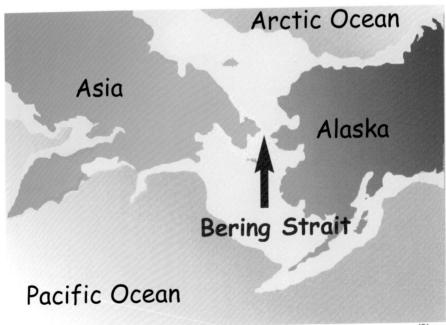

Graphic (P)

Paleoindians

Eventually, by around 13,000 B.C., some of these people reached the Ohio Country (long before it was ever named "Ohio"). This was during an Ice Age.

Paleoindian spear points come in a variety of shapes and sizes.
Graphic (Q)

People who lived very long ago are called Paleoindians. The word paleo means "old." Very large animals, like mastodons and mammoths (huge, furry elephant-like animals), lived then, too. The Paleoindian people hunted these and other animals. They probably gathered nuts and berries, too.

How do we know about these people if they didn't write? Some other evidence has been found. Spear points and stone tools have been uncovered [see graphic (Q)]. These were made of flint, a hard rock that has sharp edges when it is broken. Ohio was a good source of flint for these people. The next age after the last Ice Age is named the Stone Age

because of the importance of stones, especially flint, in the people's lives.

There is evidence that these hunters lived in caves in the Ohio region. They did not build homes because they had to keep moving, following the animals they hunted. Archaeologists, scientists who dig in the earth to find fossils and relics of ancient people, found skeletons of mastodons and other large animals in Ohio from this Ice Age. They found human skeletons and flint weapons near some mastodon skeletons. That tells scientists that Paleoindians hunted these huge beasts. Today their skeletons can be seen in museums such as those in Cleveland and Columbus.

As the glaciers melted and moved further north, these large animals became extinct. None of them survived. The Paleoindian people disappeared, too. Only their tools and weapons stayed behind in Ohio. The land held these fossils until modern scientists found them.

During the Ice Age, Paleoindians hunted a variety of big game animals including caribou.
Graphic (R)

Archaic People

Many centuries passed before another group of people appeared in the Ohio area. Known as the Archaic People, these people were also hunters who had migrated from the north and west into this region. They may have arrived as early as 7000 B.C. They used flint-tipped spears to hunt smaller animals, such as deer, bear, and wild birds [see graphic (S)]. The Archaic People also fished. Archaeologists in Ohio have uncovered ancient piles of shells, showing that these people also ate freshwater clams.

This is a selection of spear points and knives used by Archaic hunters and gatherers.

Graphic (S)

The Archaic People were more advanced than the Paleoindians. They moved in groups instead of as individuals. They lived in small villages near rivers. They cooked their food, something the Paleoindians did not do. This means they used fire, an important improvement in the development of a group of people. Charcoal, which lasts for thousands of years, was found at their excavated campsites, places that were uncovered by digging away the earth that covered them. This proves that the Archaic People had fire. Archaeologists have found items made of bone, shells, and flint at these excavation sites.

Some of the Archaic People buried their dead in gravel hills left by the glaciers. These hills are called kames. This group of Archaic People are known as Glacial Kame Indians.

The Archaic People occupied this area for more than 6,000 years. They disappeared around 1000 B.C.

Archaic people began to trade for things they could not find in their own back yard. Copper is not found in Ohio, so the Archaic Indians traded with the people who lived around Lake Superior to get it.

Graphic (T)

The Adena

Around 900 B.C., the Woodland Period began. It lasted for more than 2,000 years, until about 1200 A.D. Scientists divide this time into the Early, Middle, and Late Woodland Periods.

Graphic (U)

The people who lived in the Ohio region during the Early Woodland Period are called the Adena. They got their name when archaeologists found their remains near Adena, the Thomas Worthington Estate, in Ross County. The Adena lived in Ohio for about 1,000 years, mostly in the southern river valleys of the state.

The Adena did something that earlier people did not. They built burial mounds. These are hills in which their dead were buried, along with some of their possessions. Thousands of Adena mounds have been found in Ohio. Some are large, and some are small. The largest one is in Montgomery County. It is the Miamisburg Mound, which is sixty-eight feet high, nearly as tall as a seven-story building. The mound covers three acres of land. Today you can visit many prehistoric mounds across Ohio.

The Adena mounds help us to know a lot about the people themselves. Objects

Along the Ohio Trail

How would you feel if you went without a name for about 3,000 years? That's what happened with the Adena people. No one knew about them until 1902, when archaeologists found a tomb made of logs in a mound in Ross County, Ohio. Inside was a very, very old skeleton and some weapons and ornaments. Other skeletons and artifacts of the same period have been found in Ohio's valleys, too. No one knew who these people were.

An estate called Adena had been formed almost 100 years earlier, in 1803 when Ohio became a state. This estate belonged to a man named Thomas Worthington, who lived in Ross County, near Chillicothe. He named his estate Adena, which means "beautiful city" in Hebrew. Because of the archaeological discovery in 1902, these ancient people were named the Adena.

Here's a bit of trivia for you: Look at the Great Seal of the State of Ohio. The scene on the seal is a view from this same estate — Adena, in Ross County [see graphic (U)].

called artifacts have been found in the mounds. Some carvings show us how the Adena looked and what they wore. We also know that they lived in villages and did not move often. These people were not only hunters and gatherers, but also farmers. They built circular homes and lodges. Adena artifacts tell us that they used copper, but copper is not common to Ohio. That means the Adena probably traded flint for copper. We also know they were traders because Adena arti-facts have been found as far away as Vermont and Wisconsin.

Burial mounds are not the only mounds the Adena built. They also built effigy mounds. An effigy is an object of some kind that is made to look like someone or something. These effigy mounds were not used for burying the dead. Instead, these mounds were shaped to look like something. Perhaps they were part of the Adena's religious ceremonies. The most famous Adena effigy mound is the Great Serpent Mound [see graphic (BB) page 16], found in Adams County. This mound is 5 feet high and 1,330 feet long. It is shaped like a big snake getting ready to swallow an egg. You can see the whole mound by climbing an observation tower and looking down at it.

No one knows why, but the Adena and their culture disappeared between 100 A.D. and 300 A.D.

Hopewell
100 B.C.- 500 A.D.
This carving of a Hopewell shaman dressed as a bear was discovered within a mound at the Newark Earthworks.
Graphic (W)

This is an artist's reconstruction of a typical village of the Adena culture. *Graphic* (V)

The Hopewell

Another group of hunters, gatherers, and farmers lived in Ohio about 2,000 years ago. The Hopewell people were here from about 100 B.C. to 600 A.D. Like the Adena, they lived mostly in the southern Ohio river valleys. The Hopewell were named for Captain M. C. Hopewell, the person on whose land their remains were first uncovered. The Hopewell farm was in Ross County, Ohio, the same county where the Adena remains were first found.

The Hopewell people spread farther than the Adena had. Some of their remains have been found in the lands of northern Ohio, too. They made beautiful artifacts, different from the Adenas'. That is one way that archaeologists know the Adena and Hopewell were two different people, even though at one time they both lived near each other. The Hopewell traded these artifacts, flint, and stone used for making pipes. We know that they traded as far away as Florida and the Atlantic coast. Some items found in Hopewell sites, places where archaeologists dig for artifacts, include bear claws and a special rock called obsidian from the Rocky Mountain area. Obsidian is a very hard rock that comes from volcanoes.

The Hopewell changed the look of Ohio's land in some places. They built mounds and walls made of earth in geometric shapes: circles, rectangles, and octagons. These shapes were so well done that scientists believe the Hopewell had surveying skills. They may have been the first surveyors in Ohio. Surveying is an important skill when studying land. Surveyors are people who use math to chart the earth's surface and to mark boundary lines. They measure the land so

Along the Ohio Trail

Take a look at this town. Would you be surprised to find out that it is called Circleville? The Hopewell built two circle-shaped mounds, one within the other. When the town was established, the leaders decided not to disturb the mounds. Two of the main streets in Old Circleville Village were named Circle Alley and Circle Street. Today the city of Circleville is the main city in Pickaway County.

plans can be carried out for building things. To create their geometric earthworks, the Hopewell would have used measuring skills like this.

The most famous earthwork of the Hopewell is Fort Ancient [see graphic (Y)] in Warren County. Wall-like structures like this one were probably built for religious ceremonies, not really as forts for protection. The walls of Fort Ancient are 3.5 miles long and surround more than 100 acres. Within its walls are burial mounds, stone walkways, and moon-shaped mounds. It was the largest prehistoric construction in the U.S. You can visit this site today. Other Hopewell sites can be found in Newark, Marietta, Portsmouth, and Hamilton County.

Although the Hopewell were an advanced people, their culture disappeared, too, around 600 A.D. They were the last advanced people to live in the Ohio region until the Europeans began to arrive in the 1600s.

The walls of Fort Ancient, as seen from the south. It is located in Warren County, Ohio.

Graphic (Y)

The Fort Ancients

The Fort Ancient people did not build Fort Ancient. As you have already read, the Hopewell did. However, the Fort Ancients are named after this grand earthwork because they lived in the Fort Ancient region beginning in 1000 A.D., after the Hopewell had disappeared. The Fort Ancient culture was similar to that of the people in Mexico, like the Aztecs and Mayans. Possibly some natives migrated from there to the Ohio region. Evidence of the Fort Ancients shows that they were gone by the mid-1600s. Most anthropologists believe that the Fort Ancients may have been the ancestors of the Shawnee people.

Woodhenge, Stubbs Earthworks, Warren County, Ohio (based on excavations conducted by Dr. Frank Cowan and the staff of the Cincinnati Museum Center during the summers of 1998 and 1999).

Graphic (X)

The Hopewell Site, Ross County, Ohio.

Graphic (Z)

Paleoindian
13,000 to 7000 B.C.

Archaic
8000 to 500 B.C.

Woodland
800 B.C. to A.D.
1200

Adena Culture
800 B.C. to A.D. 100

Hopewell Culture
100 B.C. to A.D. 400

Late Woodland Culture
A.D. 600 - 1200

Late Prehistoric
A.D. 1000 to 1650

Fort Ancient culture
A.D. 1000 to 1650

Whittlesey People
A.D. 1000 to 1650

Graphic (AA)

The Whittlesey People

The last group of prehistoric people to live in the Ohio area are called the Whittlesey people. They were named for Charles Whittlesey, a geologist and archaeologist who studied prehistoric sites in northern Ohio. That is where the remains of these people were found. They lived in northern Ohio about the same time as the Fort Ancients lived in southern Ohio.

By the time the European explorers arrived in the Ohio Country, almost no people lived here. The end of the prehistoric period is marked by the arrival of these explorers. From this point, written records were

Along the Ohio Trail

Do you wonder how these ancient people moved from place to place? First of all, none of them had horses. Horses did not arrive in America until the Europeans came. They brought the animals over with them so they could move about easily in the new land.

There were two main sources of transportation: walking and canoeing. Natives walked as they hunted and moved their villages. To travel greater distances over lakes and rivers, they built canoes from young trees and branches. These frames were covered with bark and any cracks were filled with sticky resin from pine trees. Canoes helped the natives trade with other people far away. They were able to move heavy loads and many objects this way.

One of the few effigy mounds in Ohio, Serpent Mound is the largest and finest serpent effigy in the United States. Nearly a quarter of a mile long, Serpent Mound apparently represents an uncoiling serpent. Serpent Mound lies on a plateau overlooking the valley of Brush Creek. Nearby conical mounds contained burials and implements characteristic of the prehistoric Adena people (800 B.C.-A.D. 100).

Graphic (BB)

available and history could be recorded.

The prehistoric people of Ohio did not destroy the land. They lived and died here, but did not cut down, burn, or clear many trees. Other than the mounds they built, these people left the Ohio lands unchanged.

This shows an artist's view of a typical Late Prehistoric village of central and southern Ohio. You can see the ruins of older villages which were abandoned when the nutrients in the garden soils became used up. *Graphic* (DD)

This is an artist's idea of what the Hopewell people looked like.
Graphic (CC)

page 16

Native Americans, Explorers, and Traders

So many changes came with the arrival of the European explorers and traders. Before they landed on the shores of America and moved inland into the Ohio region, no one "owned" the land. The Native Americans who had lived and died here had no concept of land owner-ship. They believed that the land belonged to everyone. It was a sacred thing to them. These early people respected the land and the creatures that lived on it. That is why the Ohio region was so unchanged for such a long time. Their earthworks remind Ohioans of a time when the people belonged to the land.

That would change in the 1600s and 1700s. As more people, "invaders" from Europe, came into Ohio Country [see graphic (EE)], the race began to claim land for king and country. The new people saw the land as an object to be owned and controlled. Remember: The Ohio Country was a large area that stretched from western Pennsylvania all the way west toward present-day Illinois, north to Lake Erie, and south to the Ohio River.

Graphic (EE)

Graphic (II)

Native Americans in Ohio

Because we have written records about the Native Americans in Ohio after 1600, they are called historic tribes. Most of what we know about them was written by the French and English who explored, trapped, traded, or settled in the Ohio Country during the 1600s and 1700s. These "white men" had a lot of contact with the natives in the area, mostly because of the trading between the groups. The Ohio Country was a rich land that provided food, furs, salt, and other natural resources to both the natives and the Europeans.

No historic native tribes settled in the Ohio region until the early 1700s, but this land was a great hunting ground for many tribes. They hunted and gathered food, but did not build settlements here. The land stayed as it had been for cen-turies because no permanent changes were made to create settlements for these people. No one knows why natives did not settle in Ohio during this period, but it is likely that the strong Iroquois group from the New York area kept this region from being inhabited. The Iroquois were warlike people who fought

Along the Ohio Trail

How Natives Used Ohio's Land

The native hunters, gatherers, and farmers of the Ohio Country knew how to use the land wisely. When they hunted, they used as much of each animal as possible. Very little went to waste. Deer was a chief source of meat, but it was also important for clothing. Even shoes were made of deerskin. Natives also rubbed deer fat on their skin to keep the mosquitoes from biting! Other animals that were hunted were bears, rabbits, ground hogs, foxes, and wild turkeys.

Remember the salt licks in the first section? Women of the tribes went to salt licks, springs of salty water, and gathered the water they needed. They boiled this water until only the salt remained. Then they rubbed the salt into the fresh meat they had. The salt preserved the meat so it would not decay or spoil. Have you ever eaten beef jerky? This is meat preserved by drying.

Trees were used for making homes. Wigwams and longhouses were built from Ohio timber. Also, honey and syrup were gathered from trees. Bees made hives in hollow trees and natives scooped out the honey with their bare hands! The sap of maple trees was used to make syrup. We still eat honey and maple syrup today.

Farmers planted corn, beans, pumpkins, gourds, and tobacco for their own use and for trading. They gathered apples, berries, and wild cherries, too.

Most natives believed that the wind, water, and land had a spirit. The people celebrated nature by having ceremonies to thank the spirits for the harvest or to ask for success in planting and hunting. They played drums and flutes made from natural objects like gourds and reeds.

The natives did not believe they owned the land. Instead, they were grateful to the land for providing so well for them.

with other tribes and drove them from their lands.

The **Wyandots** were a native group that had been pushed out of their homeland of Ontario, Canada, by the Iroquois. The Wyandot tribe is also called the Huron (the French name for them). They arrived and settled in the northern part of the Ohio Country, mostly near the Sandusky area. They established the town of Coshocton. Today Wyandot County, Wyandot Creek, and several townships named Wyandot carry their name.

The **Miami** tribe came in from another direction: west. Originally from the Wisconsin region, they were pressured to move south and east by other tribes. The Miami settled in the eastern Indiana and western Ohio regions by the 1740s. They had traded with the French for many years, and much of what we know of them today comes from diaries of French missionaries. The name "Miami" is first recorded as the name of a fort (Fort Miami) built in 1685, near present-day Fort Wayne, Indiana. The chief village of the Miami in the Ohio Country was called Pickawillany. Today the city of Piqua is near there. Eventually the Miami people sold the claims to their land in Ohio and moved further west into Indiana, Kansas, and Oklahoma. Three Ohio rivers have been named after this tribe: the Great Miami, the Little Miami, and the Maumee (which was originally called the Miami of the Lake). Miamisburg and Miami County,

Along the Ohio Trail

Tecumseh was one of the greatest Native American leaders of the Ohio Country. He was born of the Shawnee tribe in 1768. The legend of his birth says that the night he was born a comet, or "shooting star," streaked across the sky. His parents, Chief Pucksinwah and Methotasa, named him Tecumseh, meaning "panther passing across." Stories were told about how he had special powers, the ability to have great knowledge.

Tecumseh was a very wise leader. He traveled from tribe to tribe in the territories of Ohio, Michigan, Indiana, Illinois, and Wisconsin trying to form a "united nation" of tribes. He believed that this larger group could keep the white man from taking over these regions. This great leader was killed in 1813 during a battle between the British and Americans.

Only one white man was allowed to draw his portrait. This is the only picture made of Tecumseh while he was living. You can find lots of interesting information about him in your school and local library.

Blue Jacket

Less is known about the Shawnee chief, Blue Jacket, than about any other Native American who played an important role in Ohio's history.

The Shawnee leader, Cornstalk, was born in western Pennsylvania about 1720. His Indian name was Holokeska.

Cornstalk

Logan

By 1770, Logan had moved his family to Ohio. He had also become a leader of the Mingo people.

Little Turtle, war chief of the Miamis, defeated Josiah Harmar (1790) and Arthur St. Clair (1791).

Little Turtle

Pontiac

It is believed that the Ottawa chief, Pontiac, was born in northwest Ohio about 1720.

The Prophet was born as Lalawitheka in March 1778 at Old Piqua on the Mad River near present-day Springfield, Ohio. His father was an important Shawnee war chief.

The Prophet

Tarhe

Tarhe was a member of the Porcupine clan of the Ohio Hurons. Ohio Hurons were also called Wyandots. Tarhe was often referred to as "the Crane."

By his early twenties Tecumseh had become a Shawnee leader. He & his brother, The Prophet, had a dream of a unified Indian nation.

Tecumseh

Graphic (FF)

of course, are also named for them.

The **Shawnee** were a proud, strong tribe of people. No one is sure where they came from, but there is good evidence that their ancestors were the Fort Ancient people mentioned earlier. We know that many settled in Ohio from Pennsylvania, but some may also have come from some southern regions. In fact, the name "Shawnee" means "people from the south." They considered Kentucky's land to be sacred and never settled there. Hunting was allowed, but no permanent residence. When Europeans started to build settlements there, the Shawnee were very angry so they often raided those villages. Just across the Ohio River, the Shawnee established settlements near present-day Portsmouth and upwards into the Scioto Valley area. Their central meeting place was called a "chillicothe," from which the city gets its name. Tecumseh was born during one of their meetings to discuss the problems with the white men. He would become one of their greatest leaders. The Shawnee and Miami tribes became allies to try to keep the white men from taking their land, but after the Shawnee leader Tecumseh was killed, the tribe weakened. They gave up all of the Ohio lands and moved into Missouri, eventually joining many other tribes in the Indian Territory of Oklahoma.

Many of the tribes that would eventually make a home in Ohio started out in the eastern part of America. Some Europeans lived in harmony with the natives, especially in Pennsylvania, but as more and more Europeans arrived, the native tribes were pushed further west. That is how the **Delaware** came to inhabit an eastern part of the Ohio Country.

Besides the Wyandot, Miami, Shawnee, and Delaware, a few other tribes migrated to the Ohio Country, too. They include the Mingo (a name that included Senecas, Cayugas and other Iroquois), Ottawa, Chippewa (Ojibwa), Kickapoo, Potawatomi, and Cherokee tribes. Even with all of these different people coming and going, questions about who "owned" the land did not come up until the European explorers "discovered" and claimed parts of the New World, including the Ohio Country. As you will see, the conflicts between the French and British are about who owned and controlled the land. Used by both sides, the native tribes found themselves involved in these conflicts, too.

Along the Ohio Trail

Ohio offered a lot of wildlife to the traders and settlers. All they needed of furs, meat, and other materials could be found without much trouble. Ohio wasn't just a natural paradise. Some dangers existed around most every tree or bush.

Wild animals were just that — wild! Livestock were attacked by bears, wolves, and wildcats. Rattlesnakes and copperheads, some of the most poisonous snakes in the world, lived in great numbers in Ohio Country. The Indians even had a belief that the plentiful raccoons of the winter changed into snakes during the summer.

Even with all that danger, the natives found a way to live in peace with the land. They used roots, plants, and tree bark to make medicine for healing their wounds or sicknesses, and their medicines worked better and were safer than the ones that were brought in later by the Europeans.

DANGER!

The French in Ohio Country

When Jacques Cartier, a French explorer, found and named the St. Lawrence River in 1534, it was just a matter of time before the French traveled up that river into the Great Lakes and finally to the Ohio Country. Explorers like Cartier found much more than land as they explored. They met many native people and discovered the riches of this land — especially the furs that were so plentiful.

In the early 1600s, the French had worked out an arrangement with the natives, especially in the Canadian regions. Explorers had moved on, but traders had moved in. They built trading posts where the French exchanged European products (like guns) for furs. In Europe, American furs were highly desired. They made hats, coats, and other objects from the fur of bears, beavers, otters, raccoons,

foxes, muskrats, and minks, all of which thrived in the Ohio area.

The Iroquois did their best to keep the French out of the Ohio Country. Even so, some explorers did reach the Ohio River. Robert La Salle is thought to have been the first white man to see the upper Ohio River, but some historians disagree with that claim. The French claimed much of the Ohio Valley because of La Salle's expedition. Many trappers and traders came

One of the plates claiming French ownership of the Ohio Country that was buried by Celeron on his expedition in 1748.

Graphic (GG)

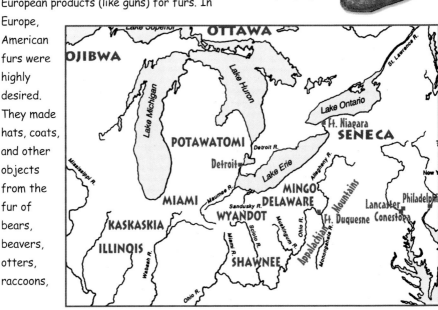

Map shows native areas and white towns around 1760.   *Graphic* (HH)

here, too, after hearing La Salle's description of the area.

The French leaders decided to build forts to protect their claims. However, none of these forts were actually built in the Ohio region. They were mostly in Pennsylvania, Canada, Illinois, and Indiana. The French never had a strong place in the Ohio Country, even though they had claimed all of Ohio for France.

The British in Ohio Country

The French moved into the Ohio region from the north (Canada), but the British came from the east where they had already established strong settlements. One main difference between the French and British was that the French mainly wanted to use the land for what they could get out of it — products for

Along the Ohio Trail

Have you planted a lead plate lately? Lead is a metal that is soft and easily carved. The French carved official declarations into plates made of lead [see graphic (GG) page 22]. They used these 11-inch x 17-inch plates to declare that the French owned the land of Ohio Country.

When the French found out that the British were trading with the natives in this area, they warned the British to leave the French territory. Of course, the British kept on trading. They had worked out a good arrangement with the natives, and the tribes preferred British goods to the French goods.

As the argument over the land and trading continued, a Frenchman named Celeron DeBienville was sent to the Ohio River area to try to get the natives to change their minds, and to bury the lead plates along the riverbanks. The French leaders felt that these "declarations of ownership" would secure the French claims to the land. Near each buried plate, Celeron fastened a thin metal plate to a tree. This small plate stated that a formal claim had been planted nearby.

Altogether, six lead plates were buried. Two have been found. One was found near Marietta, Ohio, by two boys who were swimming. The story says that they melted part of the plate to make homemade bullets.

For all his work, Celeron was completely unsuccessful. The natives still traded with the British and the French had almost no presence in Ohio Country.

trading. The British, however, also wanted to settle on the land, to make it their own.

The British had a big advantage over the French. The Iroquois tribes became allies with the British, but the British needed to have the Ohio tribes join the alliance. They sent three traders — Conrad Weiser, George Croghan, and Andrew Montour — to meet with representatives of the Miami, Shawnee, Delaware, Wyandot, and other tribes. This meeting was held at Logstown, Pennsylvania, on the Ohio River in 1748. After trading many gifts, the natives agreed to trade with the British. Another large group of Native Americans was on the side of the British, and against the French.

Land Disputes Lead to War

Long before the French and British came to America, they were at war with each other. In Europe, they had been enemies for hundreds of years. So it was no surprise when they competed for trade and land in the New World.

As more forts were built near the Ohio Country, it was clear that warfare there between the French and British was just around the corner. In 1753, as a last effort to ask the French to leave the area, George Washington, a well-known surveyor, was sent from Virginia to warn them to leave their forts at once.

Washington took Christopher Gist with him as he set out on his assignment to warn the French. Gist wrote about the entire trip. The French at Fort Le Boeuf, on the upper Ohio (Allegheny) River, received Washington and treated him well. The commander of the fort agreed to send the message to the French leaders in Canada, but told Washington that British traders would still be taken prisoner if they traded in the Ohio Country.

One thing was clear: the Ohio Country was going to

Ottawa

Wyandot
Upper Sandusky

Wapakoneta
Lewistown
Miami
Piqua

Mingo

Delaware
Newcomer's
Town

Shawnee
Lower
Shawnee
Town

Graphic (II)

belong only to the French or the British — not both, and only a war would decide who had the right to claim the area. That war is known as the French and Indian War.

The next year, 1754, the French and their Indian allies captured a British fort and renamed it Fort Duquesne, after the governor-general of New France. The French use of the fort was effective, and the Ohio Valley was no longer open to the British.

George Washington then led a small army to the area, was defeated and quickly established Fort Necessity. A group of French and Indians attacked the fort before it was completely built, and Washington was forced to surrender. He and his troops were allowed to return to Virginia.

Along the Ohio Trail

Natives in Ohio at the beginning of the French and Indian War could see that the French were getting stronger in Ohio Country, so they became dependent on the French for trading and protection. Shawnee, Delaware, and Wyandot warriors fought for the French near Fort Duquesne.

The French encouraged the native warriors to attack isolated British settlements further east. Many men, women, and children were killed or captured by Ohio's natives on behalf of the French. Not all captives were hurt, though. Young people were usually treated well and were even adopted into the tribe. Native families took care of them and taught them their ways.

Mary Campbell was one of these captives. She was taken from her home by the Delaware and was adopted into a native family. Seven years later, she was returned to her family in Pennsylvania.

The Treaty of Paris 1763 and the Quebec Act

The war ended in 1759 when the British, who had been very successful in taking forts in the Ohio and Mississippi Valleys, took the key French fort at Quebec in Canada. The French were completely defeated. France and England continued fighting in Europe, so the war was not officially over by treaty until 1763. The Treaty of Paris of 1763 stated that the French gave up all land rights in North America.

King George of England declared in the Quebec Act that the Ohio Valley and Great Lakes region belonged to the natives as their hunting grounds. None of this land was to be settled or purchased. Clearly, the British were trying to work with the native tribes in peace in order to preserve the valuable fur trade.

Native American Uprisings

Although the British won control of the Ohio Country, land battles between the British colonial settlers and Native Americans continued. Even though the king of England had set a boundary (called The Proclamation Line) telling his people not to settle in the Ohio Country, settlers came anyway. The natives saw the British as invaders because they wanted to own the land.

British settlers were in danger from Native American attacks. Because England had spent so much money fighting the French and Indian War, the king decided the country could not afford to send many soldiers into the wilderness to protect the settlers. At one time generous to the natives, the British stopped giving them gifts. Trading slowed down. The Ohio natives found their supplies of gunpowder and ammunition were running out. Without these, they could not hunt for food. Their very existence was being affected. Understandably, the natives became afraid — and angry.

Before European Trading (items they could make)	After European Trading (items they must buy or trade for)
spears, bows and arrows	guns and gunpowder
stone tomahawks	iron hatchets
animal skins	woven cloth, wool
clothing, wampum	glass beads
moccasins	alcohol

A native chief named Pontiac decided to organize a large group of natives, a nation of Native Americans, to push the British back over the Appalachian Mountains and out of the Ohio Country. For months, groups of warriors attacked British posts, including Fort Sandusky. British troops moved into this territory to stop the natives' attacks. Eventually peace was established with the Ohio tribes. England wanted to renew trade with Ohio's native tribes, knowing there was money to be made.

Treaty of Fort Stanwix

In 1768 the Iroquois Nations and the Ohio natives signed a treaty with the British. The Treaty of Fort Stanwix set aside land (in reserve) for these Native Americans in the Ohio Country, as well as in parts of Pennsylvania and New York. The word "reservation" comes from "reserved lands."

Though some settlers disagreed with both of these official statements, overall the Quebec Act and Treaty of Fort Stanwix were followed.

Ohio Land Claims 1770-1785

When the British signed the Treaty of Fort Stanwix in 1768, they did so with the thought of keeping peace with the Indian tribes. The treaty was supposed to reserve land and provide hunting grounds in the Ohio Country for the Indians living there, as well as establishing boundaries for settlers. However, land companies wanted to establish settlements on these lands. Some lands were even to have been granted (given) to men who served in the French and Indian War, as payment for their military service. Native Indians watched the settlers carefully, fearing the tribes would once again be moved out — or worse.

One settler group was different, though. Some Christian missionaries were welcomed into Ohio. In the 1750s, a group of Moravians (the Christian missionaries) began scouting the land near the Tuscarawas and Muskingum Rivers. By 1772, new missions had been established there. Moravian leaders and their

Along the Ohio Trail

The treaty guaranteed that these lands would not be disturbed by white settlers, but the white man did not keep his word. As settlers continued to move into the land reserved for the natives, the attacks on their settlements continued, too.

White men killed natives, too. One native leader, Chief Logan, reported that his entire family had been killed by white men for no reason.

Chief Logan gave a famous speech about this. He explained that he was "on the warpath" until he had fulfilled his revenge: to get one scalp for each member of his family who had been killed. When he took the last scalp, later Chief Logan turned back to peace.

Christian Delaware Indian followers (who will be discussed later) moved from Pennsylvania into new settlements in Ohio: Schoenbrunn (meaning "beautiful spring"), Gnadenhutten ("tents of grace"), and Lichtenau ("fields of light"). These Christian settlers and Indians lived peacefully with the Delaware already living in Ohio. The first churches and schools in Ohio were set up by the Moravians in these villages. Unfortunately, the peace of the Moravians and native Indians would not last long.

At this time colonists, residents of the thirteen colonies, were having trouble with England's rules. They resented having to live by rules set up by a government so far away and so out of touch with life in America. They especially disliked being told not to settle in areas that seemed to offer them so much: good farm-land, good hunting and trapping, and lots of land to use as they pleased. So, the colonists ignored England's laws and treaties with the Indians and began moving into the regions of Ohio and Kentucky in great numbers.

Afraid of losing their lands and angry at the broken promises, the native Indian warriors attacked the settler villages on the edge of the frontier. Many settlers and Indians were killed during these attacks. Such was life at that time on what was the western frontier of our country.

Fighting between settlers and Indians continued, and the settler leaders knew they needed to do something before the situation got completely out of control. In the spring of 1774, Lord Dunmore, the British governor of Virginia, led a group of 1,000 men down the Ohio River. Another army led by Andrew Lewis fought a group of Shawnee Indian warriors at Point Pleasant in a long and tiring battle that Lewis eventually won. Both armies then moved west into the Hocking Valley and to Pickaway, where Shawnee villages were. Dunmore established peace with the Shawnee, promising to leave the natives north of the Ohio River in peace if whites could settle south of the Ohio River without being attacked or threatened.

Portrait of a Delaware Indian.
Graphic (JJ)

Ohio Country during the American Revolution

The American Revolution was fought mostly in the East, but the Ohio Country played its part, too. The British encouraged the Indians in the frontier areas to attack the American settlers. Henry Hamilton, the British commander at Detroit, even gave the Indians rewards for bringing him the scalps of Americans. He was nicknamed "the Hair Buyer." Together the British and Indians raided frontier settlements and took many Americans as prisoners of war. The Americans knew they needed to send someone into the Ohio Country (which was really part of Virginia at the time) to protect their people. One of the most important leaders in the Ohio region was George Rogers Clark, who won victories over the British soldiers and their Indian allies. Although Clark's victories were in modern Illinois and Indiana, they helped American colonials secure the Ohio Country.

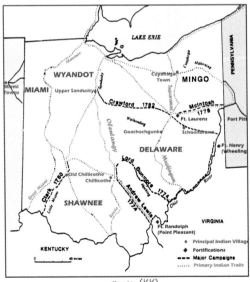

Graphic (KK)

Along the Ohio Trail

The Native American Indians in Ohio were not savages, like some old books and movies show them to be. They respected life, land, and nature, but they knew they needed to protect their lifestyle when settlers threatened to take over Ohio. The Indians, just like any race or culture, were mostly good people. There were good Indians and there were bad Indians. The same was true with the settlers.

"Good settlers" were men like Simon Kenton and Daniel Boone. Even when these men took up arms against the Indians, as stories go, they fought with fairness and honor. Though enemies, each side respected the other. In fact, both of these men were friends of several tribes at various times in their lives.

Along the Ohio Trail

Simon — that's my name. It is also the name of two men who were important in Ohio history during the American Revolution: Simon Girty and Simon Kenton. These two Simons, however, were on opposite sides of the war.

Simon Girty was raised by Native Americans after his home in Pennsylvania was raided when he was 15. He was taken into Ohio Country and he learned about the ways of the Indians. When he was freed, Simon Girty helped the British as an interpreter because he could speak the languages of the Indian tribes.

Simon Kenton was from Virginia, but moved into the Kentucky region when he was 15. The Shawnee Indians and Simon Kenton respected each other. During the war, Simon Kenton worked for the American side.

Today, Simon Girty is seen as a traitor for working with and defending the British. Simon Kenton, however, is considered an American pioneer and hero. He founded the city of Springfield, and the city of Kenton in Ohio and Kenton County in Kentucky are both named for him. Today you can visit Simon Kenton's grave in Urbana, Ohio, in Champaign County.

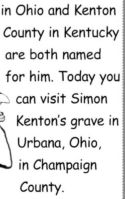

SIMON KENTON served the American Army during Lord Dunmore's War and during the Battle of Fallen Timbers where he is remembered for his bravery.

SIMON GIRTY was a skilled woodsman who was also fluent in many Indian languages. He was hated among the white settlers because he encouraged Indians to attack settlers.

The Moravian Massacre

As the American Revolution was coming to a close in 1781, the British and their Native American allies decided to move the Moravian Indians away from the Tuscarawas region. Their new home was to be shared with the Wyandot tribe near the Sandusky River. The Moravians and their Indian followers were distrusted because they were pacifists, not involved in the war. The white Moravian leaders were taken away by the British and were tried as spies.

In 1782, some of the Christian Delaware Indians were allowed to return to their old home in order to gather food from their fields. At the same time, David Williamson and 100 men were moving into the area to punish native Indians for attacking some settlers in western Pennsylvania. Williamson and his men saw the peaceful Delaware Indians gathering corn, beans, and other crops from the fields at Gnadenhutten. The Delaware Indians trusted the white settlers, so they easily did what they were told. The soldiers made the Indians gather in the church and kneel. Then Williamson and his men murdered these peaceful people and set the church on fire. Two boys escaped and ran to warn the other villages. Today there is a village at Schoenbrunn and a museum at Gnadenhutten set up for visitors to mark these places in Ohio history [see graphic (LL)].

Hearing about this violence made other Indian tribes angry. They reacted strongly and attacked colonist settlements. The British encouraged these attacks. In June 1782, Indians of the Ohio Country had surrounded a group of American soldiers under the command of Colonel William Crawford, a friend of George Washington. Many men were killed and Colonel Crawford was executed in revenge for the attack on Gnadenhutten, although Crawford had nothing to do with that attack. Today Crawford County is named for him.

The Moravian church founded Schoenbrunn ("beautiful spring") in 1772 as a mission to the Delaware Indians. The settlement grew to include sixty dwellings and more than 300 inhabitants who drew up Ohio's first civil code and built its first Christian church and schoolhouse. *Graphic* (LL)

Colonial Land Claims

The Treaty of Paris 1783 ended the war and gave the new United States territory to the Mississippi River. West of the Mississippi, however, the land was claimed by Spain.

Before and after the war, four of the new states — Virginia, Connecticut, Massachusetts, and New York — claimed land in the Ohio Country and beyond. That is because the land that had been granted to them while they were still British colonies described their western boundaries to be "as far west as land extends."

One of the first problems the new United States government had to solve was to establish clear boundaries for these new states.

A new way of thinking was needed: to think of America as a nation instead of thirteen separate state governments. During the American Revolution, a congressional committee had come up with the idea that the colonies all cede, or give up, their western lands to the new Central Government. Eventually four new states let go of their claims in the Northwest Territory — New York in 1781, Virginia in 1784, Massachusetts in 1785, and Connecticut in 1786 and 1800 [See "Settling the Ohio Lands 1787-1800, page 42].

The Northwest Territory [see graphic (MM) page 33] was the property of the new central government of the United States of America with some special conditions. Virginia had given up the most by ceding its claims — nearly two-thirds of the Ohio Valley. In return, Virginia was allowed to keep about 4.2 million acres of Ohio land between the Little Miami and Scioto Rivers. This land was called the Virginia Military District, because the land was to be given to Virginia soldiers who fought in the American Revolution. Connecticut was also allowed to keep a tract of land in northeastern Ohio. It was about 3 million acres and was called the Connecticut Western Reserve. Today Case Western Reserve University and Western Reserve Academy are named for this land grant.

Native American Land Claims

With the American Revolution over and a new treaty in place, the native Indians in the Northwest Territory had been practically forgotten. The Quebec Act had promised them land, but the Treaty of Paris 1783 did not even mention these natives. The British gave land to the new American nation that they had already agreed to give to the native Indian tribes. Now it was up to the new American government to create treaties with the Indians.

Three treaties were signed that reserved lands for the native Indians.

The Treaty of Fort Stanwix (1784) settled an agreement with the Iroquois of New York. In Ohio, the Treaty of Fort McIntosh (1785) and the Treaty of Fort Finney (1786) were made with northern Ohio tribes and with the Shawnee in southwestern Ohio. No white settlements would be allowed on the lands reserved for these tribes. The Ohio tribes rejected all of these treaties. The British continued to interfere in the area and kept problems stirred up between the tribes and the new nation, hoping the Americans would not be able to hold on to the territory.

The Northwest Territory included the land north of the Ohio River and east of the Mississippi River. *Graphic* (MM)

The Public Land Act of 1785

When the American Revolution was over, the new government had no money — but it had land. To pay soldiers for their service, the government gave a soldier a land warrant as payment. A warrant is a claim (ownership), in this case to a certain number of acres in the western territory. These warrants differed according to how long a man served in the military and what his rank was. If the soldier died in the war, then his family received the warrant for his land. The warrants in the Virginia Military District (VMD) were for areas from 100 acres to 15,000 acres.

Describing specific pieces of land was not easy. The boundaries were unclear because no consistent method had been established for marking tracts of land. Areas of land are called parcels. Most parcels were only described as a certain amount of land (a number of acres) in a general region.

Members of the new Congress knew that the land parcels in the western territories needed to be described more precisely. Congress passed the Public Land Act of 1785. They recommended that land be marked in areas shaped like squares. The Earth's surface is round and not flat, so parcels would not be perfectly square, but they could be close.

The land in the Northwest Territory was to be surveyed and divided into tracts of land six miles square (6 miles x 6 miles), called townships. Then each township would be divided into 36 sections, each being 1 mile x 1 mile square. Each township and each section was assigned a number so it could be identified. One square mile was equal to 640 acres of land. Land would be sold for $1 an acre or $640 a section. Within each township one section was to be saved, not sold, in order to provide money to support new schools. In many townships, this was Section 16 [see graphic (NN)], near the center of the township. This system of

A Township

6	5	4	3	2	1
7	8	9	10	11	12
18	17	16	15	14	13
19	20	21	22	23	24
30	29	28	27	26	25
31	32	33	34	35	36

Congress reserved section 16 near the middle of each township for the use of public schools.

Graphic (NN)

measuring and marking land for public use is known as the federal survey system. It was first used in eastern Ohio in an area just west of the Ohio River. This survey was called the Seven Ranges.

Other Ohio surveys soon followed. One of them set the Ohio-Indiana state line, called the "First Principal Meridian." The main latitude line to intersect, or cross, that longitude line was set at the 41°N Latitude. Once these two lines were established, surveyors began to set boundaries and describe the land in relation to them. Permanent markers (usually metal stakes and pins in the ground) would be laid, and boundaries could be proven. This system of surveying land was carried into many other American lands, too, as the country grew. Grids were not always established in 6-mile x 6-mile sections, but the rectangular system was imitated because it worked so well.

Along the Ohio Trail

A surveyor is someone who takes measurements of the land and sets markers to show boundary lines. He or she cannot use things like rivers, trees, rocks, or other land forms to do this because they change over time. Instead, a surveyor uses the surface of the Earth.

The Earth's surface is described by using two sets of lines: longitude lines (which run north and south) and latitude lines (which run west and east). These lines make a kind of grid over the Earth's surface, like an invisible "net" that hugs the planet.

The central longitude line (marked as 0° Longitude) is called the Prime Meridian and runs through Greenwich, England. Longitude lines that run nearly parallel to the west of the meridian are measured as °W and those that run nearly parallel to the east of the meridian are measured as °E.

The central latitude line (marked as 0° Latitude) is called the Equator and runs around the world through South America and Africa primarily. Latitude lines that run parallel to the north of the equator are measured as °N and those that run parallel to the south of the Equator are measured as °S.

A single, tiny spot on the earth can be measured using these lines. That spot can be named and recorded as the place where a latitude line and a longitude line cross. For instance, Columbus, Ohio, is 40°N Latitude, 83°30'W Longitude. Always name the latitude line first, longitude line second.

The Role of Government

Without a central government, decisions about land ownership could not have easily been made. Americans wanted to own property. Good records needed to be established and maintained so any disputes about land claims could be settled. By creating the Public Land Act of 1785, the government made a way for people to own land and to know exactly what land they owned. Today you can still see the effects of this important act when you look at a land deed for most parcels of land in Ohio.

However, the new government had more work to do. After establishing the method of surveying and mapping the Northwest Territory, Congress next needed to set up ways to govern that territory and make a way for new states to be created.

Bounty Land Warrants for Veterans of the American Revolution	
Acreage by Rank*	
Major General	1100 acres
Brigadier	850 acres
Colonel	500 acres
Lieutenant Colonel	450 acres
Major	400 acres
Captain	300 acres
Lieutenant	200 acres
Ensign	150 acres
Non-Commissioned	100 acres
Soldier	100 acres
Surgeon	400 acres
Surgeon's Mate	300 acres

*Source: William Donohue Ellis, The Ordinance of 1787: The Nation Begins, Dayton, Ohio: Landfall Press, 1987, p. 28

Graphic (OO)

Measuring from the meridian (the north-south line) and the base line (the east-west line), surveyors laid out ranges which were north-south rows of townships (from east to west of the meridian), and townships (from north to south of the base line). Each "township" consisting of thirty-six square miles was divided into 36 "sections" of one square mile each. Surveyors numbered the units of land in order to provide accurate identification of ranges, townships, sections and subdivisions within a section.

The Northwest Ordinance of 1787

Establishing government in the Northwest Territory was important to the new nation for many reasons. First, the frontier had to be strong enough to withstand any attempt by England, France, or Spain to retake the land for themselves. America's organized territories needed to have organized fighting units, or militia, for protection. British troops were still close by, and they weren't sure the new government would really last. The British wanted to control the land to help their Ohio Indian allies. The new American nation would have to prove it was strong enough to keep the territories that the Treaty of Paris had given it.

The new government also had some serious financial problems. Organizing new territories so land could be easily sold gave the leaders a way to raise money for the national treasury. Similarly, soldiers who were getting more and more upset about not being paid for their service during the war could be given land. War leaders, like George Washington, were especially concerned about these angry soldiers. He wanted them to be rewarded for their sacrifices during the war. Free land and a new beginning were all the government could afford to give them.

Finally, establishing new territories would be a way to strengthen a federal government that seemed to be getting weaker all the time. The thirteen states (formerly

A Section of Land, 640 Acres

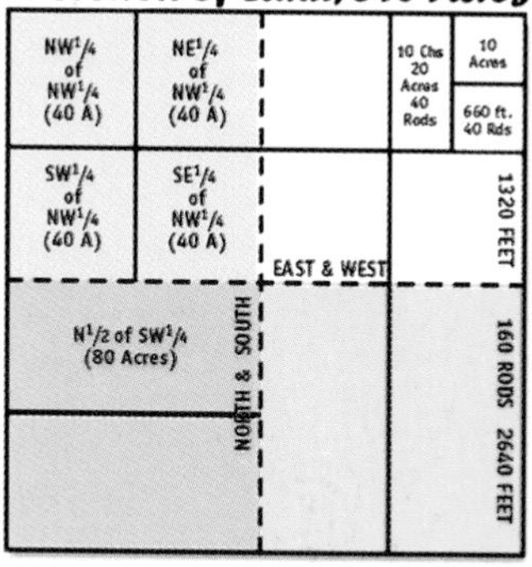

NW¼ of NW¼ (40 A)	NE¼ of NW¼ (40 A)		10 Chs 20 Acres 40 Rods	10 Acres
SW¼ of NW¼ (40 A)	SE¼ of NW¼ (40 A)		660 ft. 40 Rds	1320 FEET
N½ of SW¼ (80 Acres)	EAST & WEST			160 RODS 2640 FEET

Each section contained 640 acres. A section was divided into 160-acre quarters. More surveying divided the quarters into farms and town lots.

Graphic (PP)

colonies) were squabbling with each other. They acted as if they were separate little countries. This could not continue if the United States of America was to survive. The states and federal government needed to work together to grow a new nation.

As you have read in the previous section, parts of the western territory were ceded to the federal government by the states that had claimed the land. Therefore, the Northwest Territory became public domain, meaning it was owned by the people of the United States through their federal government. As public domain, this territory would be governed by the Congress. The Congress would decide the best way to divide the land, to settle the land, and to govern the land. The federal survey system (36-square-mile grid) was adopted as the method of surveying and charting public domain lands.

The Importance of the Northwest Ordinance

It is said that the three greatest documents in American history are the Declaration of Independence, the Constitution, and the Northwest Ordinance of 1787. In fact, much of the Constitution came about as a direct result of writings in the Northwest Ordinance. The Bill of Rights (the first 10 amendments of the Constitution) actually had its beginning in the six articles of the Northwest Ordinance.

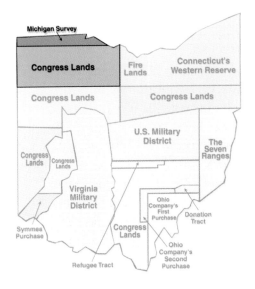

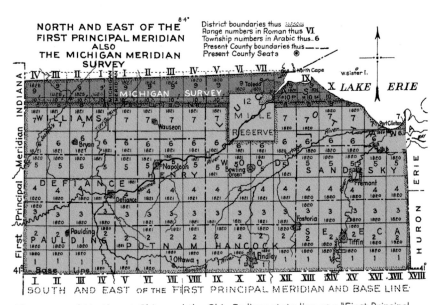

The survey of Northwest Ohio used the Ohio-Indiana state line as a "First Principal Meridian." The 41st parallel of north latitude became an intersecting, east-west base line used in surveying.

Graphic (QQ)

Some of these similarities include:

- freedom of religion
- trial by jury
- no cruel or unusual punishment
- freedom from slavery or involuntary servitude

New states would come into the nation easily because of the ordinance. Ohio would be the first to come from the Northwest Territory. Later, four more would come from this territory (Indiana, Illinois, Michigan, and Wisconsin). One of the most important effects of the ordinance was that each new state would enter the nation completely equal to the older states. Never before in the history of the world had this been done. The Northwest Ordinance became a strengthening force in the forming and growth of this nation. The Northwest Ordinance stated some important ideas and rights. Here are some examples:

- Ownership of the land was passed down to the owner's descendants. Some people died before their land warrants were used. The ordinance made a way for a veteran's family to keep the land that was promised to him.

- Governors would govern the territory; first by being appointed by Congress; then by being elected when enough people lived there. Today, each of the 50 states has a governor as its executive leader.

- A secretary would keep track of all legal records for the territory and would send copies to the Congress. A Secretary of State is an important office that remains in effect for all states today.

- Judges would be appointed to settle disputes between residents in the territory. This made sure that every American's rights would be protected no matter where they lived.

- Eventually a legislature would be elected for the region. The state legislature is the lawmaking part of the state government. Once the Northwest Territory had at least 5,000 free males

Along the Ohio Trail

Who wrote the Declaration of Independence? Mostly Thomas Jefferson, of course.

The Northwest Ordinance did not have one author. It didn't even have a dozen. Over time, this document had the input of many men as it was written and rewritten and passed through committee after committee until it took its final form.

All of the writers were careful of one thing: that they didn't write anything that sounded like something the British would have written. They replaced the words "colony" and "colonial" (though the Northwest area was certainly a colony of the new government) with "territory" and "territorial."

We still use that language today. Puerto Rico, Guam, and the Virgin Islands are U.S. territories — not colonies — and we have many others. All but 20 of our 50 states were territories before becoming states. The exceptions are the 13 colonies, California, Kentucky, Maine, Texas, Vermont, Tennessee and West Virginia.

over the age of 21 living there, a legislative council was formed and a house of representatives could be elected.

- The governor would be the commander-in-chief of the militia.
- The governor would appoint (choose) sheriffs to protect the citizens. Ohio still has sheriffs in most counties, but they are now elected rather than appointed.
- The governor would arrange for surveys of the land as needed.

A constitution was the last of three steps needed for a territory to become a state. (The first was the appointment of a governor, secretary, and three judges; the second was the forming of a house of representatives.) A constitution could be drawn up (written) once a region had 60,000 inhabitants. After revisions and final approval of its constitution, the territory could apply to the federal government for statehood. Any states coming into the nation would be on "equal footing" with the original states (some of the

leaders of the original states were not especially happy about this part). Most state constitutions are similar to each other. The Northwest Ordinance tells how a state will be governed and what rights the citizens can enjoy:

- Civil and religious freedoms were to be protected. Civil rights (rights as citizens of the United States) and religious rights (freedom to worship however one wants) are among the most important parts of the ordinance.
- Every person would have rights in court.
- Waterways leading to the Mississippi River and St. Lawrence Seaway would be forever free of taxation.
- Provisions were made for no fewer than three and no more than five states in the Northwest Territory. As we know, five states were created from this territory.
- Slavery was prohibited. The ordinance stated, "There shall be neither slavery nor involuntary servitude in said territory." Nearly 100 years later, after the Civil War, the Thirteenth Amendment to the United States

Along the Ohio Trail

Can you see how the ideas in the Northwest Ordinance have affected Ohio?

Who is the governing leader of Ohio today?

Do we have a state legislature?

Who represents your area?

Does your county have a sheriff?

On what side was Ohio during the Civil War?

Why?

Constitution would repeat almost the same words — ending slavery in the United States.

• Education was encouraged.

The Legacy of the Ordinance

A legacy is something that is left for the future by someone or something. The legacy of the Northwest Ordinance was a nation that reached "from sea to shining sea." Before this ordinance, there was no method by which a territory could become a state. With this ordinance, not only was a method adopted, but it was a method that worked well. As the nation grew, the method made the path smooth.

It would not run over the natives to do so. One section of the ordinance stated that:

"The utmost good faith shall always be observed toward the Indians. Their lands and property shall never be taken from them without their consent; and in their property, rights, and liberty, they shall never be invaded or disturbed unless in just and lawful wars authorized by Congress."

Unfortunately, years later, the last part of this section was used to justify (make an excuse for) taking lands from them in Ohio, but especially in the Great Plains and farther western lands.

So, with the method ready, the nation was set to go — into the Northwest Territory to grow the nation.

Along the Ohio Trail

Most early settlers wanted to live in the woodland areas. Because these people were farmers, they believed that this was the best land for growing crops. They figured if trees grew there, then crops would, too.

Before they could plant anything, they had to clear the land. There were two ways to remove the trees: cutting them down or killing them. The settlers girdled the trees. They cut away some bark from the tree all the way around, like a belt of missing bark. Soon the tree would die.

Once the trees in an area had died, Farmers removed all the bushes and grasses (underbrush) so they could plow the land. They used axes and saws to cut down the trees, and the timber (wood) was used to build their cabins, fences, and other buildings. Logs would be dragged to the building site. Bark was removed and logs were smoothed out as much as possible. They cut notches in the ends of the logs so they could stack them to make the cabin's walls. Then they filled the cracks between the logs with mud or clay.

Inside, a finished cabin had either dirt floors or flat log boards to walk on. A fireplace kept the home warm, gave light in the evening, and provided heat for cooking. Families also used candles and lanterns for more lighting. A loft, an upstairs area reached by a homemade ladder, was built where the children usually slept.

The first crop of these early settlers was corn, because it was so versatile (able to be used many ways). Dried corn was ground up into cornmeal and used to make cornbread, mush, and johnnycakes — a corn pancake. Corn was fed to livestock. Some was saved as seed for the next year's crop.

Ohio's rich soils made farming successful. Today Ohio still produces great corn crops — and more!

Settling the Ohio Lands 1787-1800

One of the most helpful effects of the Northwest Ordinance of 1787 was that the government finally had clear control over the settlement of the Northwest Territory, especially in the Ohio region. Congress had tried to keep illegal settlers out, but more and more squatters, people who claimed land merely by living on it, moved into Ohio Country. Lands that had been reserved for natives were being settled, too, causing tension between settlers, natives, and the government.

Congress was concerned that westward settlement was quickly getting out of control. Forts were built and military action by U.S. troops was taken to move the squatters out. Sometimes their homes were even burned down. The squatters moved back and rebuilt their cabins. Clearly, this territory was going to be settled one way or another. By enacting the Northwest Ordinance, Congress finally had a method that would make expansion into the territory orderly and measurable.

The lands of Ohio were the first to fall under the provisions of this ordinance. Ohio became the practice area for establishing settlements, and problems were worked out. Territories that were settled next benefited from the trials and errors of settling Ohio first. Each tract of land in Ohio Country has its own survey and settlement story [see graphic (RR)].

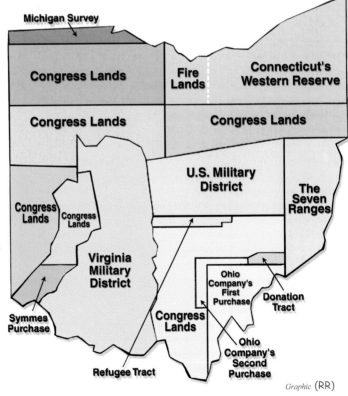

Graphic (RR)

The Virginia Military District

After Virginia gave up its claims to the largest portion of the Northwest Territory, the state was allowed to keep one portion of land. This land was between the Little Miami River (on the west), the Ohio River (on the south), and the Scioto River (on the east and north). The map on this page, graphic (SS) shows this as the Virginia Military District (VMD). As you have learned, this land was used as payment to military veterans from Virginia for their service during the American Revolution. These lands had been surveyed under an old method, not under the Public Lands Act that used the federal survey system. The descriptions of each property were often unclear and even unfair.

In order to actually claim land issued by a Virginia military warrant, the following steps had to be followed in order:

1. The veteran had to send the warrant (paper) to the person who was responsible for the surveying of the VMD.

2. Next a deputy surveyor would write a general description of the land (called an entry).

3. The deputy surveyor would run an actual survey.

4. Once the survey was accepted, the warrant was sent to the federal government.

5 The federal government would issue a U.S. patent for that parcel of land. A patent is an official document that gives the right to own the land to a specific person or organization.

Graphic (SS)

By following these steps, records could be kept of land parcels. The men who did the surveys were usually given part of the parcel (20% or more) or they were paid cash as payment for their services. Many surveyors grew rich by selling off the many land parcels they were given.

George Washington himself had a Virginia military warrant for 23,333 acres in the VMD. He did not follow through on this. At one point he had land in Clermont and Hamilton counties surveyed, but these lands were never issued a patent in Washington's name.

The first settlement in the Virginia Military District was at Manchester, just north of the Ohio River. Next the Chillicothe area was surveyed and became the population center of the VMD. Of course, many of these VMD settlers were from Virginia. Although they were allowed to have slaves in Virginia, they could not bring them into the new territory. That provision in the Northwest Ordinance held firm, and Ohio would ever be a free state.

After many years and many surveys, Virginia ceded to the federal government any land in the Virginia Military District that had not been patented or claimed. In 1871 Congress ceded this land to the state of Ohio. The next year Ohio set this land aside as an endowment (something that provides income or support for an organization) for The Ohio State University. The university was able to sell these lands in order to raise money for its ongoing growth and development in Columbus and central Ohio.

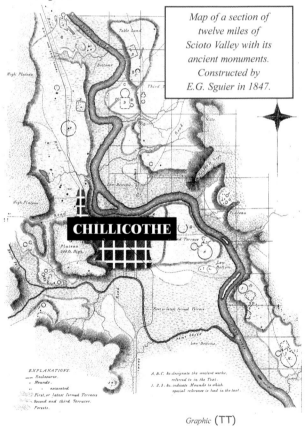

Map of a section of twelve miles of Scioto Valley with its ancient monuments. Constructed by E.G. Sguier in 1847.

CHILLICOTHE

EXPLANATIONS.
Enclosures.
Mounds.
excavated
First, or latest formed Terraces
Second and third Terraces.
Forests.

A, B, C. &c designate the ancient works, referred to in the Text.
1, 2, 3, &c. indicate Mounds to which special reference is had in the text.

Graphic (TT)

The Seven Ranges

As you can see on the map on page 46, graphic (UU), the Seven Ranges are located on the eastern boundary of Ohio. This area was the very first tract surveyed using the federal survey system under the Public Land Act of 1785. The area could not be divided into smaller sections until the western boundary of Pennsylvania (called the Geographer's Line) was established. In 1785, Thomas Hutchins, the Surveyor General of the United States, set it at about 80° 31' West Longitude (Now this is the boundary between Pennsylvania and West Virginia. North of that, the boundary between Pennsylvania and Ohio was surveyed and set later.).

Next he marked the point where the Geographer's Line touched the north bank of the Ohio River. Called the "Point of Beginning," this would be his starting point for surveying the area. The line ran west, 42 miles from the Point of Beginning (which is now in East Liverpool). A range is a vertical (up and down) row of townships. Each range was six miles wide, so seven ranges made up 42 miles. That is where the name "Seven Ranges" came from.

Even after four ranges had been surveyed, not much of this area had been sold. Congress was concerned about the

Along the Ohio Trail

One of the key men to settle the Virginia Military District was Nathaniel Massie. He was a surveyor and a land developer. A land developer is someone who plans out how an area of land can be developed to benefit the people living there. In 1790 he chose a site near the Ohio River and got nineteen other men involved in settling this area. He gave each of them lots (small sections of land) in exchange for being part of his new settlement. This was the first official settlement in the Virginia Military District. Called Massie's Station at the time, today this town is known as Manchester, Ohio.

Massie also surveyed and helped settle the Chillicothe region, northeast of Manchester.

slow sales because it needed money for the national treasury. What Congress needed was to find a group of businessmen — land developers and investors — who were interested in buying large areas of land in the Northwest Territory. Fortunately, that is exactly what happened.

Before 1796, each section of a township had to be numbered like TABLE A, starting in the lower right-hand corner. Numbering moved up. Then a new row (called a range) would continue being numbered from the bottom and up.

Today, in 29 states a legal description of a parcel of land must still contain the numbers of the range, township, section, and part of section, and the original land survey name.

The only properties to use this numbering system were the Seven Ranges, the Between the Miami Rivers Survey, and the Symmes Purchase Survey. In 1796 the numbering method changed.

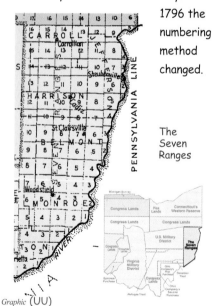

The Seven Ranges

Graphic (UU)

The Ohio Company

The Ohio Company of Associates was formed in Massachusetts in 1786. Led by General Rufus Putnam, Reverend Manasseh Cutler, Major Winthrop Sargent, Captain Thomas Cushing, and Colonel John Brooks, this group offered to buy land from Congress at just the right time. They wanted to start new lives in the new territory after the American Revolution.

Manasseh Cutler and Winthrop Sargent met with a congressional committee to discuss the purchase. Cutler persuaded the committee to sell a very large tract of land to the Ohio Company. The deal was to buy 1,500,000 acres by making a down payment of $500,000 and paying the rest of the money (another $500,000) after the surveys were finished. Major General Arthur St. Clair, the president of Congress, supported the Ohio Company's plans. The main reason he did so was that the men of the Ohio

TABLE A					
The Federal Survey System					
1785 to 1792					
36	30	24	18	12	6
35	29	23	17	11	5
34	28	22	16	10	4
33	27	21	15	9	3
32	26	20	14	8	2
31	25	19	13	7	1
Range 6	Range 5	Range 4	Range 3	Range 2	Range 1

This table shows the federal numbering system for sections within a township.
(an area of 36 sections, each section being 1 mile by 1 mile = 1 square mile).
Each township was 36 miles square
(6 miles by 6 miles).

Map of The Ohio Company's Purchase in Southeastern Ohio. *Graphic* (VV)

some during this time, the average price per acre turned out to be about $8\frac{1}{2}$ cents.

Rufus Putnam and Manasseh Cutler led the first surveyors and settlers to the first Ohio Company Purchase. Boats and rafts were built to carry the 48 men (plus an unknown number of women and children) to their new land. They left Pennsylvania on April 2, 1788, and five days later reached the mouth of the Muskingum River. April 7, 1788, is celebrated as the first day of permanent, authorized settlement in Ohio. Nearby was a fort, Fort Harmar, which would provide protection. With a fort and river nearby, this would be a good place to settle. They named their settlement Marietta in honor of the queen of France, Marie Antoinette (The French had helped the colonies win the American Revolution. This was one way to thank them.).

Rufus Putnam was in charge of the survey. Surveyors worked on laying out the town for lands outside the town. They used the method shown in the Federal Survey System table on page 46, the same one established by the Public Land Act of 1785, but because the land was so hilly, the rectangular method was not as exact as in some other later areas. In Marietta surveyors marked out commons (open areas that belonged to the townspeople), in-lots (lots in the town itself), and out-lots (farmland lots outside the town). When designing the new town, the leaders were careful not

Company had promised to support him as the first ever Governor of the Northwest Territory, and they did.

After making the first payment, the land was to be surveyed. The boundaries were east to the Seven Ranges, south to the Ohio River, west to the Seventeenth Range, and north as far as necessary to make up the entire 1,500,000 acres [see graphic (VV)]. You can see this as the Ohio Company's First Purchase (1787) [see graphic (WW)]. In 1792 the Ohio Company's Second Purchase was made. Altogether, the Ohio Company owned nearly 1,800,000 acres. Because the nation's economy suffered to disturb the native mounds that they found. A large mound can still be seen today in Marietta's Mound Cemetery.

Later, in 1792, another tract of land was granted (given) to the Ohio Company. It was called the "Donation Tract" and consisted of about 100,000 acres. The purpose of this was to make a buffer (land that serves as a protective area) between the settlers and the natives. This land was given away in 100-acre parcels to any white male who would settle on the land as soon as he received the deed to it. Many years later, in 1862, this model was used in a similar offer (free land given to the person who was going to settle on it) that was made to settlers heading west into the Plains. It was called the Homestead Act.

Far west of Marietta, in 1785-86 Major Benjamin Stites and some soldiers were led into Ohio by Simon Kenton to get back some horses that had been stolen in Kentucky by Shawnee natives. While there, Stites was impressed by the land he saw. He knew it would be a good place to establish a settlement. Today this area is in Hamilton County.

After returning home to New Jersey, Stites eagerly told his Congressman, Judge John Cleves Symmes, about the land. Symmes decided to go see the land for himself. Located between the Great Miami and Little Miami Rivers, this area was rich with potential. Symmes met with some friends back in New Jersey to discuss setting up a company to buy this land. Among these men was Jonathan Dayton. In 1788, these men decided to ask for 1 million acres to be sold to their company. Congress agreed to sell them about 330,000 acres instead because of concern over another territory and its boundaries. The Symmes Purchase, which is also called the Miami Purchase, was granted in 1788 and modified in 1792.

After following all the necessary steps, the U.S. patent on this purchase was signed by President George Washington in 1794. The same requirements were

Michigan Survey

Congress Lands

Fire Lands

Connecticut's Western Reserve

Congress Lands

Congress Lands

U.S. Military District

The Seven Ranges

Congress Lands

Congress Lands

Virginia Military District

Symmes Purchase

Congress Lands

Ohio Company's First Purchase

Donation Tract

Ohio Company's Second Purchase

Refugee Tract

Graphic (WW)

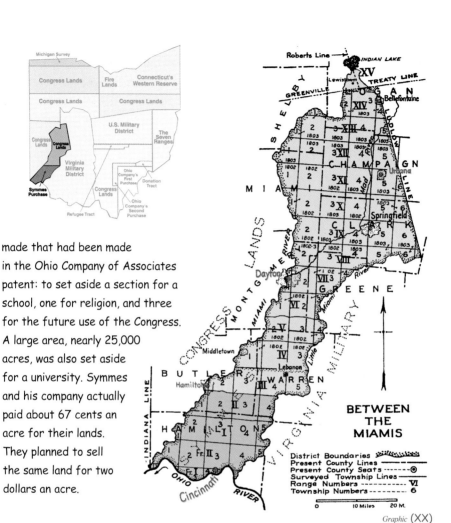

Graphic (XX)

made that had been made in the Ohio Company of Associates patent: to set aside a section for a school, one for religion, and three for the future use of the Congress. A large area, nearly 25,000 acres, was also set aside for a university. Symmes and his company actually paid about 67 cents an acre for their lands. They planned to sell the same land for two dollars an acre.

Along the Ohio Trail

Governor St. Clair named the town of Cincinnati in honor of an organization of soldiers in the American Revolution. The Society of the Cincinnati was started by George Washington himself. Its name comes from a Roman general, Cincinnatus, who (like Washington) was a farmer after a time of war who left his farm to help save the city of Rome. Washington understood this call to duty. After the American Revolution, he, too, went back to his farm at Mt. Vernon. It wasn't long, though, before he was called to serve as the leader of this new nation. President Washington eventually returned to his farm after many years of public service.

Cincinnati was the first official seat of government in the Northwest Territory.

Arthur St. Clair became governor of the Northwest Territory on July 9, 1788.
Graphic (YY)

The first man to buy land in the Symmes Purchase was Benjamin Stites himself. He led 26 men, many with families, to start a settlement near the mouth of the Little Miami River. This area would eventually be a part of Cincinnati, Ohio.

Next, three land developers from Kentucky bought land from Symmes. This tract was across from the mouth of the Licking River. One of the men named the town Losantiville (L was for Licking; os is for the Latin word for "mouth"; anti means "across from or opposite"; and ville means "city."). Fort Washington was built nearby for protection. Governor St. Clair [see graphic (YY)] came in 1790 and organized Hamilton County, declaring this new town to be the county seat (center of local government). He renamed the town Cincinnati.

Symmes himself led a group of settlers to establish the town of North Bend, near a northern bend of the Ohio River and the mouth of the Great Miami. He invited a man from Marietta, Israel Ludlow, to come with them. Ludlow was in charge of laying out the section lines in the Symmes Purchase area. This was a private survey rather than a federal one. It did not follow the established federal survey system, and much confusion has come because of it. As other lands were surveyed above the Symmes Purchase, the federal surveyors followed Ludlow's unusual method in order to keep the areas similar to each other. Many towns that were laid out by Ludlow today have streets named for him. North Bend became the home of William Henry Harrison, a future U.S. president, and the son-in-law of Judge Symmes.

Judge Symmes set aside an entire range for his friend, Jonathan Dayton. Some years later, Robert Patterson and his family moved into what is now Montgomery County and established the town of Dayton, named in Jonathan Dayton's honor.

New settlements continued to be established as more and more people came into the Ohio territory. Records show that between 1788 and 1789 more than 10,000 people came down the Ohio River, some settling at Marietta and some continuing on to other regions near Cincinnati or further north along the Great Miami. In years to follow, even more settlers moved into the rich lands of Ohio.

The Settlement at Gallipolis

The name "Gallipolis" means "city of the Gauls" (the Gauls were people during the Roman era who settled in what is now France). While most of the land companies in America were busy trying to get Americans to settle the Northwest Territory, one land company thought it was a good idea to invite Europeans to come, too. Some men realized that France was experiencing some serious problems as the French Revolution shook the country. Many French people feared for their lives, as many had already been beheaded by the guillotine. The leaders of the Scioto Company offered French citizens a chance to leave their country and start a new life in America.

Not surprisingly, the Scioto Land Company exaggerated about the land they were selling, making it seem like a paradise for settlers (They weren't the first to use this deceptive selling technique. Captain John Smith also made the New World sound much better, and easier to settle, than was true.). Lands were sold to many Frenchmen, who expected to find a wonderful new life in the lovely western lands.

In 1791 about 500 French people sailed for the U.S., thinking they owned property. When they arrived, however, they discovered that the papers they held, deeds, were completely unusable. As it turned out, the Scioto Company did not actually own any land at all. One of the members of the company took all the money, and the federal government did not grant the land because payments had not been made.

Some of the French stayed in the eastern cities, but others continued west, hoping to find what had been promised by the Scioto Company. When they arrived at the lands described in their deeds, they discovered that many of these parcels actually belonged to the Ohio Land Company. Kindly, Rufus Putnam quickly had some cabins put up, and he offered to sell the French settlers an in-lot and out-lot each in Marietta. Some agreed and settled there. Others bought land nearby from the Ohio Company for $1.25 an acre. They named their town Gallipolis.

In 1795, Congress granted (gave) another 24,000 acres "to the French inhabitants of Gallipolis." This was known as the French Grant, and was Congress's effort to let the French know that the government did not approve of how they had been treated by the Scioto Land Company.

Along the Ohio Trail

Come to Ohio ...
"the most salubrious [good for your health],
the most advantageous,
the most fertile land ...
known to any people in Europe ...
The garden of the universe,
the center of wealth,
a place destined to be the heart of a great Empire."

That's what the Scioto Company's sales pitch said.

The French people who came to Ohio were not prepared for life on the frontier. Most of them were lawyers, doctors, watchmakers, goldsmiths, shop owners, and noblemen. This upper class of people was the most in danger in France during the French Revolution. Few of them had farmed or built a home. During the first two years in Gallipolis, they nearly starved to death because they did not know how to farm. Instead of growing useful plants like corn and beans, they planted rice, almond trees, and artichokes — not the best food for a long winter. Some men were even killed when trees they were cutting down fell on them. Malaria took the lives of some, as well. Their choices were few: leave, die, or learn to survive.

So they survived. These French settlers were determined, strong-minded, and optimistic (having a positive outlook). Though many eventually moved back East, those who remained helped build a city that became known for its craftsmen. Stone carvers, watch makers, and other artisans built business and a good reputation for their work. The French, who have a love for wine, learned to make new varieties from grapes they grew, as well as peach and apple brandy.

These brave people (who, in the end, paid twice for their land — once to the Scioto Company and secondly to the Ohio Land Company) helped establish a city that still exists today.

page 52

Native Wars and the Treaty of Greenville

Even though the American Revolution was over, the British continued to be a problem for the Americans. The British soldiers did not return to England. Instead, they controlled the Canadian regions near the Great Lakes and the St. Lawrence River. They kept the natives stirred up about American settlers moving into the Northwest Territory and encouraged the natives to attack the settlements. The British even gave them guns and ammunition.

Because of these attacks, settlers needed to build forts for protection against the natives. Fort Washington was built near Cincinnati. Soon Fort Hamilton and Fort Jefferson were built in western Ohio, too. In 1790, the new governor of the Northwest Territory, Arthur St. Clair, decided to send an

One of the wampum belts presented at the signing of the Treaty of Greenville. Exchanging belts of wampum was a special way of giving your word.
Graphic (ZZ)

army to punish the natives. He asked General Harmar to head north from Cincinnati. They got as far as present-day Fort Wayne, Indiana, where the Miamis hit them with a surprise attack. Many Americans were killed, and the rest fled back to Cincinnati's Fort Washington. Next, St. Clair himself led an army. His men were defeated, too.

Concerned about these losses, the federal government helped out. In 1792 Congress sent a leader from the American Revolution, General Anthony Wayne [see graphic (AAA)], to Fort Washington

General "Mad Anthony" Wayne
Graphic (AAA)

(his nickname during the Revolution was "Mad Anthony Wayne" because of his courage and willingness to take risks). After more than a year of training, Wayne and his men moved north and built Fort Greenville (a 50-acre enclosure that was originally spelled Greene Ville) in 1793. Then they went to the area where St. Clair had been defeated and built Fort Recovery. The next spring (1794) they built Fort Defiance along the Maumee River in northwestern Ohio. This was a good name for a fort because it was built in the middle of native territory (Defiance means the act of resisting or showing opposition).

The British at Detroit knew what the Americans were doing. Natives told them all about the new forts and the growing army that was better trained than previous ones had been. Concerned that the Americans were getting too close to British Canada, the British built Fort Miami, also on the Maumee River.

Set for battling the natives, General Wayne first sent a message to

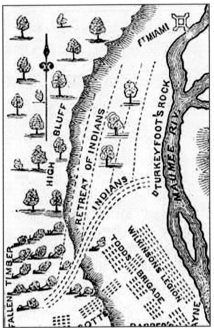

the tribes, asking them to consider meeting with him in order to avoid a fight. Reportedly, their leader Little Turtle wanted to discuss options for peace, but the other natives would not have it. Neither the warriors nor the British would listen to him.

On August 20, 1794, a battle began. In present-day Lucas County, a large area had been hit at some long-ago time by a strong wind, perhaps even a tornado. Tall trees had been blown down all around. Whites called this area "Fallen Timbers" [see graphic (BBB)]. This

This map shows the positions and movements of the American troops and the Indians during the Battle of Fallen Timbers. *Graphic* (BBB)

Along the Ohio Trail

Want to play "dot-to-dot"? Here are the actual words of the Treaty of Greenville, describing the boundary. Read it. Then, step by step, see if you can trace the boundary completely.

"The general boundary line between the lands of the United States and the lands of the said Indian tribes shall begin at the mouth of the Cuyahoga River and run thence up the same to the Portage between the Tuscarawas branch of the Muskingum, thence down that branch to the crossing place above Fort Laurens, thence westwardly to a fork of that branch of the Great Miami running into the Ohio, at or near which stood Loramie's Store and where commenced the portage between the Miami of the Ohio and St. Marys River, which runs into Lake Erie [Maumee River]; thence a westerly course to Fort Recovery, which stands on a branch of the Wabash; thence southerly in a direct line to the Ohio, so as to intersect that river opposite the mouth of the Kentucky or Cuttawa River."

You can check out some of these very sites yourself. Monuments stand at the sites of Ft. Washington, Ft. St. Clair, Ft. Jefferson, Ft. Recovery, Ft. Defiance, and even Fallen Timbers (In the town of Ft. Recovery, part of a fort has been reconstructed). Another reconstruction — of Loramie's Store — can be visited in the village of Ft. Loramie, Ohio.

seemed to the natives to be a good place to make their stand against the white soldiers. Blue Jacket was their leader, and Tecumseh was there, too, but hiding behind tree trunks was no defense against Wayne and his men. Using their bayonets, the Americans fought a short, decisive battle. Many natives retreated, running north to the British at Fort Miami for protection. The British closed the gates and the natives could not get in. Native tribes learned, once and for all, that they could not trust the British to help them.

Once again, it was time to make a treaty with the natives. General Wayne and his assistant, William Henry Harrison, met with tribal leaders at Fort Greenville in June 1795. Tecumseh, however, would not sign a treaty with the whites. More than 1,000 natives gathered at Fort Greenville to discuss the terms of the treaty. New boundaries were set between American lands (where settlers were welcome) and native lands (reserved only for them). This boundary is known as the Greenville Treaty Line. North of the line was native territory. The tribes were also promised annual payments (in cash and goods) from the American government.

Connecticut Western Reserve

You will recall that Congress had allowed Connecticut to keep a strip of land in the Ohio Country when in 1786 Connecticut gave up to the federal government its right to most of its land claims. It kept an area that reached

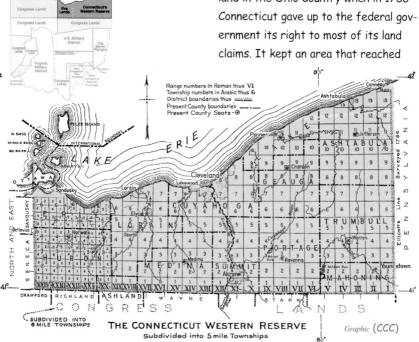

Range numbers in Roman thus VI
Township numbers in Arabic thus 6
District boundaries thus ~~~~~~~
Present County boundaries ___.___
Present County Seats ~⦿

THE CONNECTICUT WESTERN RESERVE
Subdivided into 5 mile Townships

SUBDIVIDED INTO
6 MILE TOWNSHIPS

Graphic (CCC)

about 120 miles west from the western border of Pennsylvania. It was called the Connecticut Western Reserve (or, to some, the Western Reserve) [see graphic (CCC) page 55]. If you compare that area with the new Greenville Treaty Line, you will see that the western part of this area had just been given to the natives. The natives had no intention of sharing this land with white settlers.

The state of Connecticut decided to sell the Western Reserve (but not the Fire Lands — see below) to the Connecticut Land Company in 1795. This company purchased three million acres for $1,200,000. Forty-eight men made up the company, and one of its leaders was General Moses Cleaveland. Cleaveland had served in the American Revolution and in the Connecticut legislature. He was chosen by the company to lead a surveying team to the area in order to lay out its sections. They followed the rectangular system, but the townships were set as five miles square rather than the federal system's six miles square. Most of the land near Lake Erie was rich and fertile. Land south of that area tended to be wet, swampy, steep, and hilly.

The surveyors laid out a town along the mouth of the Cuyahoga River. They named it Cleaveland (No one knows for

Ohio Townships as surveyed under the Rectangular System.

2	1
3	4

Divisions of Lots in
U.S. Military District
Graphic (DDD)

3	2
4	1

Divisions of Lots in
Fire Lands and Reserve
Graphic (EEE)

Related in surveys of 5 mi. x 5 mi. townships each divided into four lots.

6	5	4	3	2	1
7	8	9	10	11	12
18	17	16	15	14	13
19	20	21	22	23	24
30	29	28	27	26	25
31	32	33	34	35	36

Sections numbered
After Law of 1796
Graphic (FFF)

36	30	24	18	12	6
35	29	23	17	11	5
34	28	22	16	10	4
33	27	21	15	9	3
32	26	20	14	8	2
31	25	19	13	7	1

Sections numbered
Before Law of 1796
Graphic (GGG)

Related to the Basic Federal Grid of 6 mi. x 6 mi. townships each divided into 36 sections.

sure, but it is believed that at some point the letter "a" in Cleaveland's name was accidentally left out. The spelling of the town's name has been Cleveland ever since.). Other towns were also started: Warren, Youngstown, Painesville, Canfield, Ravenna, Conneaut, Poland, and Hudson. Cleaveland himself eventually went back to Connecticut and never returned to the town that held his name.

By 1797 all of the Connecticut Land Company's land had been surveyed. Settlers bought tracts and moved in. Travelers into Ohio had previously come mainly by way of the Ohio River. Now they could arrive by following water routes from Lake Ontario to the Niagara River to Lake Erie. Even heavy items, like wagons and livestock, could be transported from the East by using the larger water routes.

The Fire Lands

During the American Revolution, the British and Tories (Americans who sided with the British) invaded the colony of Connecticut. They not only attacked, but they also burned nine of the towns they invaded. Benedict Arnold, a well-known traitor, oversaw the burning of one town

himself. More than 1,800 people suffered the loss of all their worldly goods. So in 1792, the state of Connecticut decided to help these people. About 500,000 acres in the Western Reserve were set aside for these "sufferers."

The area was surveyed in five-mile square townships. Each of those townships was divided into fourths (quarters) of 4,000 acres each. Individuals drew lots (a way of choosing using chance — like randomly pulling a number from a hat) to determine which land they would receive.

The Fire Lands, or Sufferers' Lands [see graphic (HHH)] were claimed by some of these sufferers or their heirs in a company called the Ohio Corporation.

Today the Fire Lands are located in Erie, Huron, and parts of Ashland and Ottawa counties.

The United States Military District (USMD)

In 1796 the U.S. Congress set aside a tract of 2.5 million acres to take care of any outstanding military land warrants from the American Revolution (similar to the Virginia Military District, but not limited to the residents of only one state). In this case, warrants (or bounty) had been given according to rank using

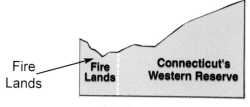

Graphic (HHH)

the same values found in the Military Bounty Table on page 36.

The USMD's [see graphic (JJJ), page 59] boundaries were the Greenville Treaty Line (north), the Seven Ranges (east), the Refugee Tract and Congress Lands (south), and the Scioto River (west). The area was surveyed in five-mile square townships because the leaders felt it would be easier to use this size and its subdivisions to match the land warrants that had already been issued. Each township was divided into fourths (quarters), like the Fire Lands, but numbered differently.

Not many veterans showed interest in this land. Often they sold their land without ever having seen it. Some traded their military land warrants for land scrip (paper used like money to buy land), which they could use for any public domain land, not just USMD land.

The United States Military District can be found in the present-day counties of Franklin, Delaware, Knox, Licking, Morrow, Noble, Marion, Holmes, Coshocton, Muskingum, Tuscarawas, and Guernsey.

The Refugee Tract

Some residents of Canada had supported the colonies during the American Revolution. They left their settlements in Canada and Nova Scotia to come to America to help during the war. These refugees (people who leave one land to find safety elsewhere) were granted land under the Act of April 7, 1798 [see graphic (III)], as long as they had left Canada before the war actually began in 1776 and had not returned to it before the war was over in 1783. In all, 67 people received nearly 60,000 acres. The tract had already been surveyed.

Today parts of Franklin, Fairfield, Licking, and Perry counties are found in this tract. Refugee Road in Columbus, Ohio, was named for it. Most of Ohio's state offices, including the Statehouse, are located in this tract.

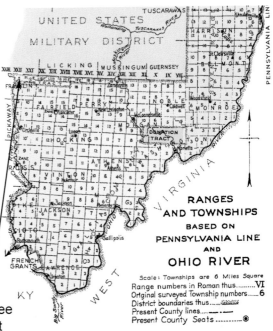

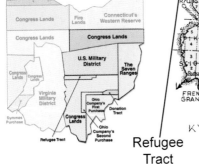

Refugee Tract

Graphic (III)

Other Land Grants

Some smaller areas were granted, or given, to individuals because of services they provided the government. One of these men was Arnold Henry Dohrman, a U.S. agent at the court of Lisbon, Portugal, during the American Revolution. While there, he made sure that American sailors who had been captured by the British were fed, clothed, and given medical treatment. He spent his own money to do this. When the war was over, Dohrman gave Congress a list of all his expenses during the war. He was repaid, some of it in cash, and the rest he received as a land grant. He was given an entire township (about 23,000 acres) in the Seven Ranges area. Half is in Harrison County; the other half is in Tuscarawas County.

Ebenezer Zane had laid out a road for the government that ran from Wheeling, Virginia (now West Virginia), through Ohio to Limestone, Kentucky (now Maysville, Kentucky). Called Zane's Trace, it opened in 1797. In exchange for his work, the Congress gave him three tracts of land, each 640 acres, which he could choose for himself. One was on the Muskingum River (now in Zanesville, Ohio), one was on the Hocking River (now in Lancaster, Ohio), and one was on the Scioto River, across from Chillicothe. Why did he choose these spots? Because of the road he had already laid out, Zane knew that these were key points where people needed to cross the rivers. Zane operated ferries at all three points. This was a good business because people needed these boats to help them cross the rivers with their goods. Zane's brother, Isaac Zane, also received three

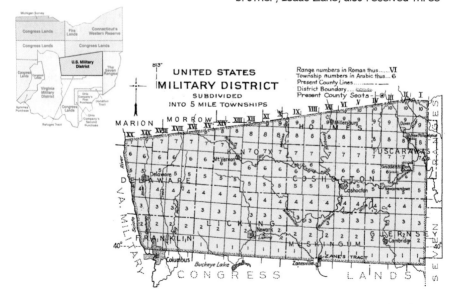

Graphic (JJJ)

sections for his services to the government. These tracts are located in present-day Champaign County.

The Congress also gave some small land grants to various natives (because of treaty agreements), to white men who had been captured and who had lived with the natives, and to some early settlers in northwest Ohio who had traded with the natives.

Later you will learn about the Michigan Survey, which was not complete until 1836.

Governing a Growing Region

By 1800, thousands of people had moved into Ohio Country. As they settled, the need to have a solid form of government was apparent. It was difficult to govern such a large territory, especially when the governor (St. Clair), judges, and secretary were required to travel so far to settle disagreements or to establish communities.

Along the Ohio Trail

Ohio's leaders saw some strange things as they traveled from town to town to check on the progress of its people. A lawyer from Cincinnati, Jacob Burnet, wrote about one such visit.

While on their way to Detroit, Burnet and his group (lawyers and judges) stopped at a native town where the chief of the Delaware tribe lived. While there, the whites watched an exciting ball game. About 100 men were playing against 100 women. The point of the game was to throw a ball between poles set at the ends of a field (like soccer and baseball combined). The field was five acres long! And the women beat the men. Says Burnet, "...a mammoth squaw...got the ball and held it, in spite of the efforts of the men to shake it from the grasp of her uplifted hand, till she approached the goal, near enough to throw it through the stakes."

Squaws – 1; Warriors – 0

Highlights at eleven.

Ohio Statehood
1800-1812

Steps Toward Statehood

You will recall that the Northwest Ordinance of 1787 set up the necessary steps for a territory to become a state. Before Ohio had achieved these steps, three other regions had already become states: Vermont (1791), Kentucky (1792), and Tennessee (1796) became the four-teenth, fifteenth, and sixteenth states.

Ohio already had its territorial governor (St. Clair), judges, and secretary — the first step toward statehood. Now Ohio needed to have its own laws, and that is what a legislature does. Up to this point, St. Clair, the judges, and the secretary had tried to select some laws, or codes, for the inhabitants to live under. Ohio's people began to complain that they

Along the Ohio Trail

How would you feel if you couldn't vote in the next big election because you didn't own any land — or you weren't a man — or you weren't white — or you were under 21? That's the way it was in the U.S. — and the Ohio area — during the early 1800s. This law had been in effect for hundreds of years in England, and it came over to America with the Pilgrims.

In Ohio's first real election (in 1799 for the territorial legislature), a man could vote only if he owned at least 50 acres of land. In order to be a member of either the house or the senate, a person had to be a male who owned at least 200 and 500 acres, respectively. Clearly, the male landowners were ruling the region, and the country. There were more people who could not vote than those who could.

The two political parties at the time disagreed about this. The Federalists thought it was okay the way it was. The newer party, strongly supported by Thomas Jefferson, the Republicans, did not want it to continue (this is not the same Republican Party that exists today). These politicians believed that we needed a more democratic system that allowed more people to vote. Eventually laws were passed that gave more and more people the right to vote.

were not being represented and that a group of five people could not adequately govern such a large territory.

St. Clair acknowledged that the second step, having at least 5,000 free adult male inhabitants, had been reached. It was time to create a territorial legislature. Elections were held over the entire territory. Delegates were chosen by the end of 1798 and met for the first time in February 1799 in Cincinnati. Most were from Ohio because this was the most populated area of the Northwest Territory. This group of men was elected to represent a large area.

Edward Tiffin was chosen speaker of the house of representatives. He would go on to become a Democratic-Republican governor of Ohio from 1803 until 1807.
Graphic (KKK)

The Northwest Territory was larger than most European countries, including England.

At the second meeting of the territorial legislature, Edward Tiffin [see graphic (KKK)] of Chillicothe was chosen as speaker of the house of representatives. Henry Vanderburgh (of Indiana) was chosen as president of the council (the council is what today we would call the state senate).

The legislature (made up of the two houses: representatives and council) got busy. They set up clear election laws and began to establish taxes so the territorial government had money with which to operate. Land was taxed at different rates, depending on how good the land was (from 85 cents per 100 acres for good land, down to 25 cents per 100 acres for poor land). County courts assessed (determined the value of) and collected the taxes. The legislature also passed laws about public service, personal behavior, and criminal activities. It also upheld the provision in the Northwest Ordinance forbidding slavery in this territory. The leaders felt that allowing slave labor into this state would undermine the development and growth that free labor could provide. They believed that slavery could severely affect the economic potential of Ohio.

Land Offices

Selling land in Ohio was a way for Congress to make money for the national treasury. Much of the land in Ohio still belonged to the federal government. You can see these areas on the map on page 42 wherever you see "Congress Lands" indicated. Since these lands were not controlled by a land company, a way to sell parcels needed to be established.

Along the Ohio Trail

Breaking the law has always been a serious offense, and in the Ohio settlements, communities had to make up their own laws. In Marietta, the leaders fastened their laws to a tree. A lawbreaker might pay a fine, have to work around the settlement, be whipped, or even be sent away from the settlement forever.

Once the territory had a legislature, then the same laws and penalties would apply in all towns. Here are some laws that were passed by the first legislature:

- **Arson was punishable by death (the territory was a very wooded land, so arson was taken very seriously).**
- **Bounties were offered for wolf scalps. Many farmers were upset about having their hogs and sheep killed by wild animals.**
- **Public cursing was illegal.**
- **No businesses could operate on the Sabbath.**
- **Gambling, dueling, fighting, and public drunkenness were illegal.**

As for public service, men were required to work on the roads of the territory. As the area developed, roadways became more and more necessary, but who was going to make them? The residents of Ohio, that's who. All "able-bodied men" had to give a certain number of days to helping build Ohio's roads. These "public workers" helped make roads and build bridges. If they didn't show up, they were fined as much as 75 cents per day!

In 1800 William Henry Harrison [see graphic (LLL)], who had been serving as secretary to the Northwest Territory and who had just been elected as a delegate to Congress, came up with a good plan. His plan was accepted by Congress and was named the Harrison Land Act, or the Act of May 10, 1800. It called for land offices, places of business, to be established in Steubenville, Cincinnati, Chillicothe, and Marietta. Individuals interested in buying federal land could go to one of these offices to find out about the land and to make their purchases. A person no longer had to be part of a land company to get a good deal on land.

According to Harrison's plan, land could be bought on credit. This also helped individuals who were not wealthy become landowners. The buyer would put down five percent of the cost of the land (which included the fees to survey the land) on the day of the sale. Then another 20 percent had to be paid within 40 days. A total of 25 percent had been paid up to this point. Finally, the owner would make three annual payments of 25 percent each within the second, third, and fourth

In 1800 William Henry Harrison, served as secretary to the Northwest Territory. He would go on to become the 9th President of the United States (March 4, 1841 to April 4, 1841).

Graphic (LLL)

years. Those payments had a six-percent interest attached to them, encouraging owners to pay off their land debt more quickly.

The price of the land was arrived at by public auction. All those who were interested in a parcel of land would bid on it. The person with the highest bid would win the right to purchase the land at that price. The minimum parcel was set at 320 acres.

Within the land office, two main positions were created. The Receiver of Public Monies handled the financial details of collecting the money for the land. The Registrar was the person who recorded the transactions (Thomas Worthington, brother-in-law of Edward Tiffin, was in charge of the land office in Chillicothe). Once a buyer paid for his land, the Registrar issued him a final certificate. This certificate was then sent to Washington, D.C., so its U.S. Patent could be issued. This sometimes took a long time to complete. The President himself had to sign every patent (until 1833). Then the patent was returned to the land office from which it originated, and the owner received it. Interestingly, many people never picked up their patents. The land office in Chillicothe still had thousands of unclaimed patent papers when it closed in 1876.

The first land office was officially opened in July 1800 in Steubenville, Ohio [see graphic (MMM) page 65]. Over the next 20 years, nearly 9 million acres of Ohio land were sold.

Dividing the Territory

Because of its great size, leaders knew the Northwest Territory would have to be divided before any part of it could be a state, but where should the dividing line fall? This became a strong political issue, affected by political parties and personal interests. Some people wanted the area to be split at the Great Miami River, allowing the eastern half of Ohio to become a state and the western half to remain as a less-governed territory. Governor St. Clair wanted to divide it at the Scioto River, mainly because he wanted to split up his political enemies and create two completely separate governments. He was also trying to keep Ohio from attaining statehood. He vetoed one law after another (which as governor he could do) to keep this from happening.

Photograph of the Marietta Land Office building. *Graphic* (NNN)

Leaders from Chillicothe opposed this idea. Led by Thomas Worthington, they went to Congress with a proposal to keep the divisions that were indicated in the Northwest Ordinance. Worthington is regarded today as the "father of Ohio statehood." The town of Worthington, near Columbus, is named for him.

On May 7, 1800, Congress agreed with the group from Chillicothe and divided the Northwest Territory along a line that ran from the mouth of the Kentucky River north to Fort Recovery and continuing north to Canada (later when the state is formed, the line is changed to begin at the mouth of the Great Miami and running north to the Michigan line). The land east of the line was still called the Northwest Territory, with Cincinnati as its capital; the land west of the line became the new Indiana Territory, which included the present-day states of Indiana, Illinois, Michigan, and Wisconsin. William Henry Harrison was chosen as the new territory's governor.

Ohio Land Offices

- Toledo
- Cleveland
- Defiance 1848-1855
- Tiffin 1828-1832
- Akron
- Youngstown
- Lima 1835-1843
- Upper Sandusky 1843-1848
- Bucyrus 1832-1842
- Canton 1808-1816
- Wooster 1816-1816
- Wapakoneta 1833-1835
- Marion 1837-1845
- Steubenville 1800-1840
- Delaware 1820-1868
- Piqua 1820-1833
- Dayton
- Springfield
- Columbus
- Zanesville 1804-1840
- Chillicothe 1801-1840
- Marietta 1800-1840
- Cincinnati 1801-1840
- Portsmouth

Graphic (MMM)

The Enabling Act of 1802

With steps one and two already achieved, the next step was only a matter of population growth. As you recall, the Northwest Ordinance established that once a section of the Northwest Territory had 60,000 people living there, it could begin the process of applying for statehood. In 1800, Ohio's population reached about 45,000 (Native Americans were not counted in the census — an official count of people — because they were not citizens and did not pay taxes). Over the next two years, the population did grow.

Leaders of the Ohio region moved quickly to ask Congress to create a new state here. Congress agreed, knowing that by the time the group had a state constitution in place the population would have reached the 60,000 mark.

On April 30, 1802, President Thomas Jefferson signed into law the Enabling Act of 1802 (as in, enabling the territory to become a state). The ordinance established the state's boundaries and gave its people the right to draft a constitution. Its language is very similar to that of the Northwest Ordinance. The preamble, or opening statement, of the ordinance states:

> An act to enable the people of the eastern division of the territory northwest of the river Ohio, to form a constitution and state government, and for the admission of such a state into the union, on an equal footing with the original states, and for other purposes.

The Enabling Act also stated that the counties could send representatives to Chillicothe to select a name for the state and to write the state's constitution. Section 16 of each township was to be set aside for education [see graphic (NN) page 34]. The Congress granted that the salt springs located in present-day Licking County would be owned by the new state. Finally, it set aside part of Michigan to become part of the new Indiana Territory.

Ohio Map in 1803 when the state was admitted to the union.

Graphic (OOO)

Ohio's Boundaries

The Enabling Act of 1802 established the soon-to-be state's boundaries as: "bounded on the east by the Pennsylvania line, on the south by the Ohio river, to the mouth of the Great Miami river, to the west by the line drawn due north from the mouth of the Great Miami..., and on the north by an east and west line drawn through the southerly extreme of Lake Michigan...and thence...through Lake Erie, to the Pennsylvania line..."

This description is not as specific as it needed to be. Later Ohio would have to settle some land disputes because of some uncertainty about the boundary, especially to the north regarding Michigan's boundary and to the south regarding rights on the Ohio River.

Along the Ohio Trail

There was no mistaking Governor St. Clair's view on making Ohio a state. He had governed the Northwest Territory from the beginning, and in some ways he could not move on with the times. He would have no power in this new state, and as he grew older, he became grumpier and less effective as a leader.

As the new territorial legislature met to discuss Ohio's future, St. Clair asked to speak to the group. Many did not want to hear what he had to say, but one of his enemies suggested they listen — because he thought St. Clair might just say enough to get himself in big trouble.

Guess what? He did. He ranted and raved about how Congress had no right to pass a new law that affected this territory. He even told the group to just ignore the new law. Before long, President Jefferson himself heard what St. Clair had said. Jefferson dismissed St. Clair from office and sent a replacement right away. Charles Willing Byrd, the man who handed St. Clair his dismissal papers, was his replacement.

His angry last years overshadowed the great work he had done for the Northwest Territory. In 1818, poor and living in an old log cabin in Pennsylvania, Arthur St. Clair died.

GOVERNOR ST. CLAIR DISMISSED

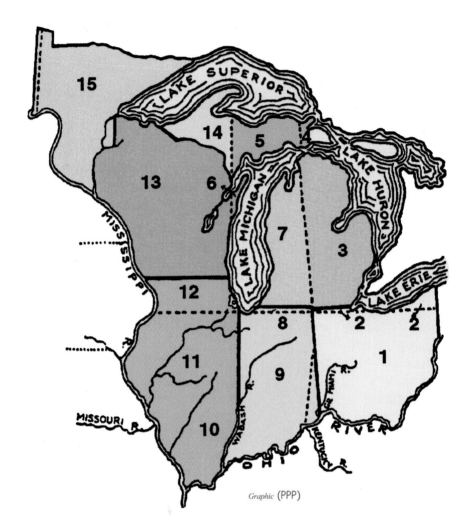

Graphic (PPP)

Map of the Northwest Territory

The Ordinance of July 13, 1787 provided "...there shall be formed in said territory, not less than three nor more than five states..." The original boundaries were defined as: Eastern State (numbers 1,2,3,4); Middle State (numbers 5,6,7,8,9) and Western State (numbers 10,11,12,13,14,15). These divisions are marked by broken lines on the map.

Congress later decided to divide the Northwest Territory into the state of Ohio (1803), Indiana (1816), Illinois (1818), Michigan (1837), Wisconsin (1848), and Minnesota (1858); as shown by the heavy solid lines on the map.

Map Source: Biographical Directory - General Assembly of Ohio 1929-1930: Columbus, 1931.

Ohio's Constitutional Convention

On November 1, 1802, thirty-five men met in Chillicothe to write a constitution. This was called Ohio's First Constitutional Convention. It took them only twenty-nine days to complete. These men were some of the brightest, most able men this country has seen, and their ability to work well together made this part of the process go smoothly. Only one person of the thirty-five was opposed to statehood, so their general agreement was a great advantage.

Even so, these men decided it was best for Ohio not to submit the constitution to the general population for a vote. They felt this might put statehood at great risk because several key people were siding with St. Clair and the Federalist Party.

The constitution established that the first election in the state would be held in January 1803. For the first time in this country, someone who did not own land was able to vote. Any adult free male (and there should have been no slaves in Ohio, according to the constitution) who paid taxes could vote. The offices to be elected included: state senators and representatives, governor, sheriffs, township trustees, justices of the peace, and coroners (people who decide the cause of death of another person). The legislature of Ohio was given more power than the governor, who in fact was merely a figurehead (someone who has a title, but little or no power). This was probably in reaction to Governor St. Clair's attempts to hold too much power.

Thomas Worthington was chosen to hand-deliver the constitution to Congress. Nearly three weeks after leaving Ohio, Worthington arrived in Washington, D.C. He met with the president and on December 22, 1802, he delivered his document to Congress.

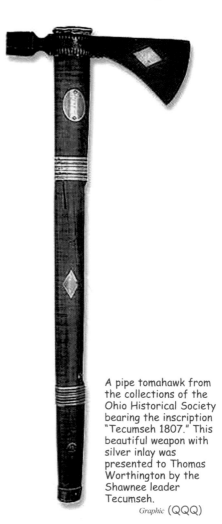

A pipe tomahawk from the collections of the Ohio Historical Society bearing the inscription "Tecumseh 1807." This beautiful weapon with silver inlay was presented to Thomas Worthington by the Shawnee leader Tecumseh.
Graphic (QQQ)

Statehood for Ohio

After consideration and approval in both houses (Senate and House of Representatives), Ohio's constitution was made official, approved by a final bill that was signed by President Thomas Jefferson on February 19, 1803 [see graphic (OOO) page 66]. Ohio was the seventeenth state of the union, although the new state legislature chose March 1, 1803 as the official date.

By this time, the January election had been held. The new governor of the state of Ohio was Edward Tiffin. No one even opposed him in the election. He was sworn into office on March 1, 1803, in Chillicothe, the first capital of Ohio.

Chillicothe remained the state's capital until 1810. Because of politics, the capital was moved to Zanesville from 1810 to 1812, when it returned to Chillicothe. Still not satisfied with this site, the state legislature considered some other options for capital cities. Four citizens from the town of Franklinton in central Ohio offered to donate ten acres on the east side of the Scioto River for state buildings and another ten acres for a state penitentiary. In 1816 the new city was named Columbus, and it became the capital of Ohio. It remains our capital to this day.

Along the Ohio Trail

Did you know that Ohio has the only flag of all 50 states that isn't a rectangle? Technically, its shape is called a "burgee," a special type of pennant. It has seventeen stars, for being the seventeenth state. The white circle inside the blue triangle represents the "O" for Ohio. The red center represents the eye of the buckeye, a state symbol.

About the Great Seal... in the very first assembly of the Ohio legislature in March 1803, leaders felt that Ohio should have an official state seal. A seal represented official government authority. Official papers would be stamped with a seal to indicate they were approved by the government. A committee was set up to design a seal for Ohio. Over the years, Ohio has had different seals. Here are some of them:

Seal of the Northwest Territory used from July 26, 1788 until Ohio statehood.

Canal scene used in the State of Ohio Seal from early 1840's to 1866.

Present Seal of the State of Ohio, as modified in 1967

Ohio's Early Leaders

Here are some early leaders and their wives. You can find much more information about them at your library.

Edward and Mary (Worthington) Tiffin. Edward was a physician who married Mary Worthington while they lived in Virginia. The Tiffins moved to Chillicothe, Ohio, in 1798, and Edward became involved in politics. He was the first governor of the state of Ohio and he served two terms. He had been asked to run for a third term as well, but chose not to do so. In 1807 he was chosen to represent Ohio as a Senator in Washington, D.C. The following year, his wife Mary died. Edward was so upset that he resigned from office. The town of Tiffin in Seneca County is named for him.

Thomas and Eleanor Worthington. Tiffin's brother-in-law, Thomas Worthington [see graphic (RRR)] (brother to Tiffin's wife Mary) and his wife decided to move to Ohio with the Tiffins in 1798. They built a stone house near Chillicothe and named it Adena. You can visit their home today and, from one view, see the scene that is depicted on the Great Seal of Ohio. Thomas helped write the state constitution. In 1803, he became one of the two first Senators from the state of Ohio. He was a well-liked and powerful member of Congress. In 1814, he left the Senate to become the fifth governor of Ohio. His wife, Eleanor, raised ten children and managed their home. Many important people came to their home, including Presidents Madison and Monroe, Henry Clay, Daniel Webster, and the Shawnee leader Tecumseh.

Samuel and Hannah Huntington. In 1801 the Huntingtons (with six children) moved from Connecticut to the Western Reserve, to what is now downtown Cleveland. A lawyer, Samuel represented Trumbull County at Ohio's constitutional convention. He was elected to the Ohio Senate and eventually to the State Supreme Court. He became our third governor, serving from 1808 to 1810.

Return J. and Sophia Meigs. Married in 1788, Return and Sophia Meigs moved from Connecticut to Marietta with The Ohio Company of Associates. They built two homes there, the second of which you can still visit today. Return Meigs served as Ohio's fourth governor, from 1810 to 1814. These were important years, as you will discover in the next section. In 1819 Meigs County was formed from part of Gallia County and named in honor of Governor Meigs.

In 1803 Thomas Worthington became one of Ohio's first senators. In 1814 he took office as Ohio's 6th Governor.
Graphic (RRR)

Although a county
may have been
established earlier,
it did not function
as a county until it
was organized.

The year the
county was
organized.
Graphic (SSS)

The year the
county was
established.
Graphic (TTT)

Ohio and the Nation 1800-1900:

A New State and the Natives

While Ohio's leaders were busy taking the steps toward statehood, Ohio's natives were growing more and more concerned about how many whites were moving in. Even though the Treaty of Greenville had promised them that settlers would not be allowed to cross the Greenville Treaty Line, the natives knew that no imaginary line had kept them out before.

They were right not to trust the treaty. In 1805 and again in 1807 new treaties were made that forced the natives to give up more land west of the Cuyahoga in the Western Reserve, land south of that to the Greenville Treaty Line, and land in northwestern Ohio. Older native leaders knew it was useless to fight against the well-armed and ever-growing white movement. Younger leaders became angry and were less likely to give in without a fight.

Tecumseh had learned he couldn't trust the British because of what happened at Fort Miami, but he trusted the Americans even less. Tecumseh's brother Tenskwatawa (known as the Prophet) [see graphic (UUU)] was the spiritual leader of the Shawnee, and the younger ones listened closely to what he had to say. He told them that he had seen a great vision of the future. He said that the Shawnee were to return to their old ways and not to follow the white man's ways anymore.

Tecumseh grew more alarmed when William Henry Harrison was appointed as governor of the Indiana Territory and set up his headquarters at Vincennes. The warrior's concern was well-founded. Within a short time, Harrison made natives sign treaties that gave away much of their Indiana homeland to the white settlers. The Shawnee leader began developing a plan that called for several tribes to unite and take a stand against the white invaders. For two years he visited tribes in Ohio, Indiana, Michigan, Illinois, Wisconsin and else-

Tecumseh's brother Tenskwatawa (known as the Prophet) was the spiritual leader of the Shawnee.

Graphic (UUU)

The War of 1812 — Ohio's Part

In spite of the trouble with the natives, Ohio grew. More counties were added as large areas divided. The largest town in Ohio was Cincinnati, a prosperous trading place because of its position on the Ohio River. By 1812, the population of Ohio grew to about 240,000.

The British continued to be a problem to the new United States. Arguments about northern boundaries and the irritation of having British-manned forts nearby kept the mood between the two countries tense. On the seas, British vessels attacked American merchant (trading) ships and forced the captured U.S. seamen to serve on the British naval ships, but to Ohioans, the worst issue was the ongoing aid of the British to the native tribes. White settlements would never be safe from attack as long as the British were supplying and encouraging the natives' attacks.

The U.S. Congress officially declared war on England on June 17, 1812. Ohio found itself right in the middle of things. Governor Meigs readied Ohio for involvement in the war, organizing a state militia. He, and many others, knew that the British, who controlled Detroit, would try to take over the new Michigan Territory, Indiana Territory, northwestern Ohio, and part of Lake Erie.

where, trying to create unity among the natives. He also set up a town near the Tippecanoe River (in Indiana) where these tribes would gather and live.

Harrison kept track of what Tecumseh was doing, and Tecumseh was well-informed about the forceful methods Harrison had used to take away large chunks of native land. At one point Tecumseh even visited Harrison to tell him that what he was doing was wrong. Harrison did not listen or change his ways.

In November 1811, Harrison and his men decided to attack the natives at Tippecanoe while Tecumseh was away gathering support in the South. Tecumseh's brother, the Prophet, was a weaker leader and was not as wise and patient as Tecumseh. The white army set up camp nearby.

The natives, under the Prophet, attacked Harrison's army just before dawn on November 7, 1811. In the Battle of Tippecanoe, many natives were killed and the rest fled to the north and west, driven further away from their homeland. Harrison had the village of Tippecanoe destroyed. When Tecumseh returned a month later, the area was deserted. Tecumseh led his remaining followers out of Ohio and Indiana into Canada, hoping to find protection with the British.

The governor of the Michigan Territory, General William Hull, led a group of 1,500 Ohio militiamen from Cincinnati and Dayton toward Detroit. They moved through Greene County, Clark County, and Champaign County, where more men joined the group. By the time they had passed through Logan, Hardin, Hancock, and Wood counties, more than 2,000 men made up Hull's militia. Although Hull had been a great leader during the American Revolution, he was now old and not well. He made some serious mistakes on his way to Detroit, mainly losing his important papers — papers that showed the plan of attack that he and his men were following. Hull and his men arrived at Detroit before the British could get there. His men encouraged him to attack the British in their posts across the river in Canada right away, but he waited too long. When the British and their native allies arrived at Detroit, Hull was frightened by the possibility of being massacred by the natives (one of his "secret" fears that had been written about in his lost papers). The British commander, General Brock, used this fear to make Hull surrender by threatening to turn loose the natives on him and his troops. Without even telling his officers, a terrified General Hull ran up the white flag in surrender, one of the most embarrassing moments in U.S. military history.

William Henry Harrison replaced Hull as commander of the western militia.

He led troops from Cincinnati on to Lebanon, Dayton, Piqua, and St. Marys. Suffering some defeats, Harrison and his men did not give up. They built Fort Meigs on the Maumee River, believing this would be an important area for them to operate from. Troops were stationed along Lake Erie. The British tried to attack Fort Meigs, but Ohioans held it and the British retreated. Many native warriors began deserting the British army. Tecumseh, however, continued to fight and was given the rank of major general.

One of the most important battles of the War of 1812 took place in Ohio at Fort Stephenson. Twenty-one-year-old George Croghan and 150 militiamen defeated more than 1,000 British soldiers and natives in August 1813, using one cannon named "Old Betsey" [see graphic (VVV)]. After an entire day of fighting, the British left their dead and dying on the field and retreated by way of Lake Erie (today you can visit a monu-

The "Old Betsey" Cannon

Graphic (VVV)

ment to Fort Stephenson and "Old Betsey" herself — at Fremont, Ohio).

The key naval battle of the war occurred near Put-In-Bay on Lake Erie in 1813. Captain Oliver Hazard Perry (only twenty-six years old) organized men and materials in Erie, Pennsylvania, to build an American naval fleet. He knew that the British had six ships on Lake Erie. In only four months, the U.S. had a fleet of nine fully armed vessels. The two navies met on September 10, 1813. Both sides knew that this could be the turning point of the war in the west. After more than three hours of intense gunfire, Perry's main ship, the *Lawrence*, was disabled.

A great leader, Perry took the ship's flag, wrapped it around him, and had his men ferry him to the next largest ship in the fleet, the *Niagara.* From that ship, he led the rest of the battle until the British commander surrendered. The Battle of Lake Erie was won by the Americans. It was the last battle fought on Ohio territory.

The last battle of the War of 1812 was the Battle of the Thames, in Canada, where the British and natives had fled after the naval defeat. Tecumseh was killed in this battle.

The war ended in 1815 with the Treaty of Ghent. This treaty set new

Main Treaties Ceding Native American Lands in Ohio

Concluded	Place of Treaty	Acres Ceded	Tribes Concerned
1795, Aug 3	Greenville, Ohio	16,930,417	Eleven Northwestern tribes.
1805, July 4	Fort Industry, Ohio	2,726,812	Ottawas, Wyandots, Chippewas, Pottawatamies, Shawnees, Delawares.
1807, Nov. 17	Detroit, Michigan	345,600	Chippewas, Ottawas, Wyandots, Pottawatamies.
1808, Nov. 25	Brownstown, Michigan	2 Roads	Same tribes as Detroit
1817, Sep. 29	Fort Meigs, Ohio	4,554,459	Ottawas, Wyandots, Chippewas, Pottawatamies, Shawnees, Delawares & Senecas.
1818, Sep. 17	St. Marys, Ohio	n.a.	Ottawas, Shawnees, Wyandots and Senecas.
1818, Oct. 2	St. Marys, Ohio	n.a.	Weas.
1818, Oct. 6	St. Marys, Ohio	297,600	Miamis.

boundaries, clearing up long-held disagreements between the two nations. The Great Lakes were to be neutral (not to be used in war by either side) and to be used for commerce, or business. America and Canada have been at peace with each other ever since.

The treaty also established reservations for natives who wanted to live in Ohio. By 1818, Ohio's Native Americans had ceded more than 25 million acres to the U.S. government.

Along the Ohio Trail

Before the Battle of the Thames, Tecumseh had told his close friends that he knew he was going to die in the next battle. Shawnee legend says that because of his premonition (an unexplained feeling about something that has not happened yet), Tecumseh wore a disguise into battle. He was concerned that the Americans might mutilate his body if they knew who he was. Tecumseh was killed in the first part of the battle. Two tales are told of what happened to his body.

The Shawnee tales say that his warriors carried Tecumseh's body away and buried it in a secret place (some say this place is in Clark County, Ohio). They did this so he could someday return and lead them back to their homeland. However, the white man's version says that his body was taken by the man who shot him and was mutilated, just as Tecumseh feared. Today, we have no way of knowing which, if either, story is true.

This is the only image of Tecumseh we have today. He let only one white man draw his portrait.

Although Tecumseh fought against the Americans in Ohio, he was greatly respected by many and was even praised for his wisdom and courage. He is considered one of the greatest Native American leaders in history.

One More Dispute — The Michigan Survey

With boundary issues settled between the U.S. and England, only one key dispute remained. Originally, a land survey gave territory in northwest Ohio to Ohio. Today this land is in Williams, Fulton, and Lucas counties, but both the state of Ohio and Michigan Territory claimed it. In 1835, these two areas nearly went to war with each other over this dispute. Ohio militia was posted on the border, ready to invade Michigan. A few small fights broke out, but no real war began. The Enabling Act that had allowed Ohio to become a state set Ohio's northern boundary to be "an east and west line drawn through the southerly extreme of Lake Michigan, running east until it shall intersect Lake Erie." This is not a very clear description of a boundary. Several surveys

Ohio Population Growth During the 19th Century

Census Year	Total Population	White Population	African American Population	Number Born in U.S.	Number Born Overseas
1800	45,365	45,028	337	n.a.	n.a.
1810	230,760	228,861	1,899	n.a.	n.a.
1820	581,434	576,711	4,723	n.a.	n.a.
1830	937,903	928,329	9,574	n.a.	n.a.
1840	1,519,467	1,502,122	17,345	n.a.	n.a.
1850	1,980,329	1,955,060	25,279	n.a.	n.a.
1860	2,339,511	2,302,808	36,673	n.a.	n.a.
1870	2,665,260	2,601,946	63,213	n.a.	n.a.
1880	3,198,062	3,117,920	79,900	2,803,119	394,943
1890	3,672,316	3,584,805	87,113	3,213,036	459,280
1900	4,157,545	4,060,204	96,901	3,698,311	459,234

were made, but one side or the other disagreed with each one. The problem finally ended in 1836 when the U.S. President approved an act of congress that both set the boundary in Ohio's favor and allowed Michigan to be admitted as a state to the U.S. In exchange for land that Michigan felt it had lost when the boundary was set (as it presently exists), Michigan was given 9,000 square miles. This is the Upper Peninsula of Michigan.

Ohio Grows Up — Population

Few states grew as quickly as Ohio. Look at how its population changed from decade to decade:

- In 1800, Ohio's total population was about 45,000.
- In 1810, that number had grown five times, to more than 230,000.
- In 1820, it more than doubled, to 580,000.

**MAP OF
THE STATE OF OHIO 1815**

Graphic (WWW)

- In 1830, it nearly doubled again, to 950,000.
- In 1840, it grew to 1,520,000.
- In 1850, it reached 1,980,000 — nearly 2 million!
- In 1860, it exceeded 2 million, reaching 2,340,000.
- By 1900, only 40 years later, the population had doubled to more than 4 million people.
- From 1800 — with 45,000 people — to 1900 — with 4,000,000 people — Ohio's population had grown about 100 times larger in just one century.

Most of this population growth came as people in the East moved into Ohio. Also, people from Europe immigrated, or moved from one country to another, to the United States, and some of these immigrants settled in Ohio. Most people in Ohio were farmers, but as years passed and cities grew, more people found other means of making a living. Ohio is still a rich farm area, but the number of farmers, as compared to other professions, is small.

Graphic (XXX)

Ohio's Lands Today

Ohio's lands have been used in different ways over the years. Areas that were once uninhabitable (no one could live there) now have cities and villages of people who might find it hard to believe that at one time no one wanted to live on their land. Advances in building have made our roads better and our homes safer.

Today you can still find people using Ohio's land as their descendants once did. Amish farmers still use horses to plow the earth.

Ohio still produces many crops and products that are important to the national economy. Though there are fewer farms in Ohio than ever before, agriculture is still important here. Today the main crops are corn, soybeans, tomatoes, and other seasonal crops such as strawberries and melons.

Manufacturing continues to be important, too. Construction is a growing industry in Ohio. As the world becomes more technologically advanced, Ohio keeps up. Many of Ohio's manufacturing plants use state-of-the-art robotics and computerized methods when producing items such as cars, trucks, and machinery.

Today Ohioans are watching carefully the effect of technology, industry, and science on the land. Pollution is a very real concern in Ohio, especially near industrial areas. Growing populations create more air pollution, water pollution, and land pollution. Landfill areas where trash is deposited grow taller and taller as Ohio grows. The environment is threatened, and agencies within the government have been created to monitor and find solutions to these problems.

As more and more farmland is sold off for construction of housing and commerce, Ohio has needed to develop conservation efforts to keep as much of our natural beauty protected as possible. Some wildlife has become endangered, including the bobcat and barn owl. Wildlife specialists are working hard to protect these and other species of animals. Recently, some good results have come about in preserving the bald eagle, river otter, and trumpeter swans in Ohio.

Ohio is a beautiful land. Today people can still see the natural beauty as they visit national and state parks, rivers, lakes, forests, and other areas of interest. Natural history museums exist in many Ohio cities. Regional festivals that celebrate the past and present of Ohio and its land are held throughout the state, usually during the summer and fall months. People in historic dress who perform the "old-fashioned" way of doing things can show us how Ohio used to be.

With deep roots and ever-reaching limbs, this Buckeye State has been a national leader in many ways. If its citizens are careful to protect its heritage, Ohio will always be a great land with a great history and an even greater future.

The Origin of Ohio's County Names

(Date in parentheses is year county
was established, it may differ
from year it was actually organized.)

Adams (1797), named for our second president, John Adams, during whose administration the county was organized.

Allen (1820), probably named for either Ethan Allen, a hero of the Revolutionary War or John L. Allen, a hero of the War of 1812. Both men were colonels.

Ashland (1846), named after "Ashland," home of the Whig candidate for President, Henry Clay, outside Lexington, Kentucky.

Ashtabula (1808), named after the Ashtabula River which meant "Fish River" in the local Indian dialect.

Athens (1805), the county is named after Athens, Greece.

Auglaize (1848), named for the Auglaize River. "Auglaize" is a Shawnee Indian word meaning "fallen timbers."

Belmont (1801), comes from the French words "belle monte," meaning "beautiful mountain," describing the hills of the county.

Brown (1818), named for Gen. Jacob Brown, a hero of the War of 1812. Georgetown, the county seat, was the boyhood home of Ulysses Simpson Grant, Civil War General and 18th President of the United States.

Butler (1803), named for Major General Richard Butler, killed during the disastrous defeat of General Arthur St. Clair by the Indians on Nov. 4, 1791.

Carroll (1833), took the name Carroll from Charles Carroll of Carrollton, Maryland, the last surviving signer of the Declaration of Independence, who died in Baltimore on November 14, 1832, at the age of 96.

Champaign (1805), is French and means "a plain," descriptive of the level land in the area.

Clark (1818), named for Brigadier General George Rogers Clark who defeated the Shawnee Indians in a battle near Springfield, on August 8, 1780.

Clermont (1800), comes from the French word meaning "clear mountain."

Clinton (1810), named in honor of George Clinton, who was vice-president of the United States when the county was formed.

Columbiana (1803), derived from Christopher Columbus and Anna.

Coshocton (1810), is an anglicized version of the Indian village "Goschachgunk" or "Goschaching" meaning "Black Bear Town" or "where there is a river crossing."

Crawford (1820), named in honor of Col. William Crawford who was burned at the stake in 1782 by Indians.

Cuyahoga (1808), named for the Cuyahoga River. Cuyahoga is an Indian word meaning "crooked," or "winding stream."

Darke (1809), named for Gen. William Darke, Revolutionary War hero.

Defiance (1845), named for Fort Defiance built in 1794 by General Anthony Wayne.

Delaware (1808), named for the Delaware Indians who came from the Delaware River area near Philadelphia.

Erie (1838), named for the Erie Indian tribe. In their Indian dialect the word "erie" meant "cat" or "wildcat."

Fairfield (1800), Arthur St. Clair, Governor of the Northwest Territory, named this county for the beauty of its "fair fields."

Fayette (1810), named for Marie Joseph Paul Yves Roch Gilbert du Motier, the Marquis de Lafayette. He served as an American Major General in the Revolutionary War and was named an honorary U.S. citizen in 1803.

Franklin (1803), named for Benjamin Franklin, printer and diplomat.

Fulton (1850), named for Robert Fulton, inventor of the steamboat.

Gallia (1803), is derived from Gaul, the ancient name of France.

Geauga (1806), the name Geauga or Sheauga was one given by the Indians to the Grand River which flows through the county. It means "raccoon."

Greene (1803), named for Gen. Nathaniel Greene, Revolutionary War hero.

Guernsey (1810), due to the fact that many of the original settlers came from the Isle of Guernsey in the English Channel.

Hamilton (1790), named for Alexander Hamilton, the first Secretary of the Treasury, 1789-1795.

Hancock (1820), named for John Hancock, President of the Continental Congress (1775-1777) and first signer of the Declaration of Independence.

Hardin (1820), named for Colonel John Hardin who was executed by the Indians while on a peace mission in 1792.

Harrison (1813), named for General William Henry Harrison, a hero of the War of 1812. First U.S. President to have lived in Ohio.

Henry (1820), named for Patrick Henry, Governor of Virginia 1776-1779 and 1784-1786; a celebrated orator of the Revolutionary War period.

Highland (1805), describes the county's terrain.

Hocking (1818), derived its name from the Indian word "Hoch-Hoch-ing" which meant "a bottle." The Hocking River flows though this county which was once claimed by the Wyandot Indians.

Holmes (1824), named for Major Andrew H. Holmes, who was killed during Major George Croghan's unsuccessful attack on Fort Mackinac (Michigan) on August 4, 1814.

Huron (1809), the name Huron was given by the French to the Wyandot Indian tribe who lived in this area.

Jackson (1816), named for Major General Andrew Jackson, who defeated the British at the Battle of New Orleans, January 8, 1815.

Jefferson (1797), named for Thomas Jefferson, statesman and Vice President of the United States, March 4, 1797 to March 3, 1801, and the 3rd President of the U.S. (1801-09).

Knox (1808), named for General Henry Knox, the first U.S. Secretary of War.

Lake (1840), named because it borders on Lake Erie; Ohio's smallest county in land area.

Lawrence (1815), named for Captain James Lawrence, commander of the U.S. Frigate *Chesapeake* during the War of 1812.

Licking (1808), derived its name from the principal stream flowing through the county. Pioneers called it the "Licking River", but it was called "Pataskala" by the Indians. The river received its name from salt licks in the area.

Logan (1818), named for Gen. Benjamin Logan, who destroyed the Shawnee Indians Mac-o-chee Villages in the area in 1796.

Lorain (1822), named after the Province of Lorraine, France.

Lucas (1835), named for Robert Lucas, Ohio Governor 1832-1836, who personally com-manded Ohio troops in the 1835 boundary dispute with Michigan. First territorial Governor of Iowa 1838-1841.

Madison (1810), named for James Madison, U.S. President from March 4, 1809 to March 3, 1817.

Mahoning (1846), derives its name from the Mahoning River. Mahoning is from the Indian word "Mahoni," meaning a "lick" or "Mahonink," meaning "at the lick."

Marion (1820), named in honor of Gen. Francis Marion of South Carolina, the "Swamp Fox" of Revolutionary War fame.

Medina (1812), named for Medina in Arabia, the town to which Mohammed fled from Mecca.

Meigs (1819), named for Return Jonathan Meigs, Jr., Ohio Governor 1810-1814 and Postmaster General 1814-1823 who lived in Marietta.

Mercer (1820), named in honor of Gen. Hugh Mercer, who was killed at the Battle of Princeton, New Jersey, on January 3, 1777.

Miami (1807), named for the Miami Indians who claimed Western Ohio and whose prin-cipal village, Pickawillany, was located near Piqua.

Monroe (1813), named for James Monroe, U.S. Secretary of State, 1811-1817, and later the fifth President of the United States, 1817-1825.

Montgomery (1803), named for General Richard Montgomery who lost his life in the assault on Quebec during the Revolutionary War.

Morgan (1817), named in honor of Gen. Daniel Morgan, who won a brilliant victory against the British at Cowpens, South Carolina, January 17, 1781.

Morrow (1848), named for Jeremiah Morrow, Congressman 1803-1813; 1840-1843, U.S. Senator 1813-1819, and Ohio Governor 1822-1826.

Muskingum (1804), is an old Delaware Indian word meaning "a town by the river."

Noble (1851), named out of respect for James Noble, a pioneer settler who first bought land in the county in 1814.

Ottawa (1840), named for the Ottawa Indian tribe. The name in their language meant "trader."

Paulding (1820), named for John Paulding, one of three soldiers who captured Major John Andre, British spy in the Revolutionary War.

Perry (1818), named in honor of Commodore Oliver Hazard Perry, who defeated the British in the naval Battle of Lake Erie, September 13, 1813.

Pickaway (1810), named from a misspelling of the tribe of Indians, known as Piqua, a branch of the Shawnee Tribe.

Pike (1815), bears the name of Brig. Gen. Zebulon Montgomery Pike, who discovered Pike's Peak in Colorado in 1806.

Portage (1808), name comes from the old Indian portage path, about seven miles in length, between the Cuyahoga and Tuscarawas rivers.

Preble (1808), named for Capt. Edward Preble, naval commander in the Revolutionary War and the War with Tripoli.

Putnam (1820), named for Israel Putnam, Revolutionary War Major General, who gained fame at the Battle of Breed's Hill, often misnamed the Battle of Bunker Hill, on June 17, 1775.

Richland (1808), named for the richness of its soil.

Ross (1798), named by Territorial Governor Arthur St. Clair for his friend, James Ross of Pennsylvania, U.S. Senator 1794-1803.

Sandusky (1820), is a derivative of an Indian word meaning "cold water." In Wyandot and Huron languages it is "Sa-un-dos-tee" meaning "water within water pools."

Scioto (1803), takes its name from the Scioto River which flows through the county. Scioto comes from a Indian word "Scionto," meaning "deer."

Seneca (1820), named for the Seneca Indians, who had a 40,000 acre reservation north of Tiffin from 1817-1831.

Shelby (1819), named for Isaac Shelby, Revolutionary War hero and first Governor of Kentucky. Counties in nine states are named for him.

Stark (1808), named for Gen. John Stark of Revolutionary War fame.

Summit (1840), derived its name for having the highest land on the line of the Ohio and Erie Canal, known as "Portage Summit."

Trumbull (1800), in the Connecticut Western Reserve, was named for Jonathan Trumbull, Jr., Governor of Connecticut 1797-1809.

Tuscarawas (1808), named for the Tuscarawas River, an Indian term perhaps meaning "open mouth".

Union (1820), named because it was formed from parts of Delaware, Franklin, Madison, and Logan counties.

Van Wert (1820), named for Isaac Van Wert, one of the three captors of British spy, Major John Andre. Actual spelling of Van Wert's name was "Van Wart." The spelling was changed due to an illegible entry in Congressional records.

Vinton (1850), named for Samuel Finley Vinton, an Ohio Statesman and U.S. Congressman, known as the "Father of the Department of Interior."

Warren (1803), named for Gen. Joseph Warren, who was killed at the Battle of Breed's (Bunker) Hill, on June 17, 1775.

Washington (1788), Ohio's first county and named in honor of George Washington, who was president of the Constitutional Convention at the time the county was formed.

Wayne (1808), named for Major General Anthony Wayne, Revolutionary War hero, later General-in-Chief of the U.S. Army 1791-1796. Defeated the Indians at the "Battle of Fallen Timbers," August 20, 1794.

Williams (1820), honors David Williams, one of three captors of Major John Andre on September 23, 1780.

Wood (1820), named after Major Eleazer D. Wood, U.S. Army-Engineers, who built Fort Meigs in 1813 while serving on the staff of General William Henry Harrison.

Wyandot (1845), named for the Wyandot Indians, the last Indian tribe in Ohio to cede their reservations March 17, 1842. They moved to lands west of the Mississippi River in July, 1843.

Bibliography

Albanese, Catherine L. *Nature Religion in America from the Algonkian Indians to the New Age*. Chicago, Illinois: The University of Chicago Press, 1990.

Anderson, Russell, H., et. al. *The Governors of Ohio*. Columbus: The Ohio Historical Society, 1954.

Collins, William R. *Ohio: The Buckeye State*. Englewood Cliffs, New Jersey: Prentice-Hall, Inc., 1956.

Ellis, William Donohue. *The Ordinance of 1787*. Dayton, Ohio: Landfall Press, 1987.

Fifer, Barbara. *Everyday Geography of the United States*. Garden City, New York: Doubleday Direct, Inc., 2000.

Flexner, James Thomas. *Washington: The Indispensable Man*. Boston, Massachusetts: Little Brown and Company, 1969.

Foster, Emily, ed. *The Ohio Frontier: An Anthology of Early Writings*. Lexington, Kentucky: The University Press of Kentucky, 1996.

Havighurst, Walter. *Ohio: A History*. New York: W. W. Norton & Company, Inc., 1976.

Howe, Robert T. *Ohio: Our State*. Cincinnati: Roblem Publishing Company, 1997.

Hurt, R. Douglas. *The Ohio Frontier: Crucible of the Old Northwest, 1720-1830*. Indianapolis: Indiana University Press, 1996.

Knepper, George W. *Ohio and Its People*. Kent, Ohio: The Kent State University Press, 1989, 1997.

Miller, Lillian B. and the Staff of the Historian's Office. *"The Dye Is Now Cast" The Road to American Independence 1774-1776*. Washington, D. C.: Smithsonian Institution Press, 1975.

Scott, Anthony. *The Story of America*. Washington, D. C.: National Geographic Society, 1984.

Stewart, J. Mark. *Ohio: Adventures in Time and Place*. New York, New York: MacMillan McGraw-Hill, 1997.

Strickler, Jim. *The American People: A History to 1877*. Evanston, Illinois: McDougal, Littell & Company, 1986.

Thom, James Alexander. *Panther In The Sky*. Toronto, Canada: Random House of Canada Limited, 1989.

Wissler, Clark. *Indians of the United States*. Garden City, New York: Doubleday & Company, Inc., 1948.

Whitcomb, Claire and John. *Oh Say Can You See*. New York, New York: William Morrow & Company, 1987.

Glossary of Terms

accessible: capable of being easily reached

anthropologist: a scientist who studies people and their cultures

appoint: to choose for a job or office

archaeologist: a scientist who digs in the earth to find fossils and relics of ancient people

artifact: a handmade object that represents a culture

cede: to give up or give away something

census: an official count of people living in an area

colonist: a person who lives in a colony; as in the Thirteen Colonies

commerce: buying and selling of goods; business

commons: open areas in a town that belong to the townspeople

conservationist: a person who is in favor of conserving our natural resources

coroner: a person (usually a doctor) who decides the cause of death of another person

county seat: the center of local government of an area

deed: a legal document that transfers ownership of a parcel of land from one person to another

effigy mound: an earthwork shaped like an object of some kind; for example, a snake

endowment: something that provides income or support for a person or organization

entry: a written description of land that serves as a record of its survey

excavate: to uncover by digging away at surrounding materials

extinct: no longer in existence

federal survey system: the system of measuring and marking land for public use that was adopted in 1785; it used a rectangular plotting system

figurehead: someone who has an official title, but has little or no power

flint: a hard rock that has sharp edges when it is broken

girdle: to cut away the bark of a tree in a complete ring, which causes the death of the tree by stopping its source of water and food

glaciated: an area where glaciers have been

glacier: a large body of ice that spreads over land

granted: gave

historic tribe: a group of Native Americans after 1600, when written records about them can be found

immigrate: to come to a new country to live

in-lot: a lot that is within a town itself

incorporated: combined to form a unified organization

justify: to make an excuse for; to have a reason for

kame: a hill made up of gravel

land grant: land that is given by government to a person or organization

land office: an official place of business where land could be bought from the government

land scrip: a special paper used like money, but only for buying land

land warrant: a paper that gave its owner claim to a certain amount of land

loft: an upstairs area in cabins used as sleeping quarters

militia: a group of people who are trained for military duty and are called upon only in case of emergency

municipal corporation: a group of self-governing people who live near each other

neutral: not favoring either side in a war or quarrel

obsidian: a very hard volcanic rock sometimes found in the Rocky Mountain area

out-lot: a lot that is outside the town, usually farmland

pacifist: a person who is against fighting or war as a way to settle a dispute

paleo-: prefix meaning "old"

parcel: a plot of land

patent: an official document that gives the right of ownership to a specific person or organization

portage path: a route over land for carrying boats or goods from one body of water to another

preamble: an opening statement that gives the reasons for the information that will follow

prehistoric: before written records were kept

premonition: an unexplained feeling about something that is going to happen

public domain: land that belongs to all the people through their government

quarry: a place where bedrock is found and cut into shapes used for building

range: a vertical row of townships

raw material: something found in nature that can be turned into something useful or valuable

refugee: a person who leaves one land to find safety somewhere else

right-of-way: a legal right to pass over another person's land

rural: descriptive of farm land

salt lick: a place where salt is deposited, usually by a spring.

site: places where archaeologists dig for artifacts

squatter: a person who claimed land merely by living on it

surveying: using mathematics to find the area, lengths, and directions for boundaries on the earth's surface and accurately showing these on paper

surveyor: someone who surveys land

till: a mix of soil and rock

timber: wood that is cut for use

township: specific land area, usually six miles square, that was subdivided into 36 one-square-mile sections

trespass: to illegally enter another person's land

turnpike: a road a person must pay to use

turnpike company: a private company that built paved roads; payment was collected as tolls from travelers

unglaciated: an area where glaciers have never been

urban: descriptive of a city

versatile: able to be used many different ways

veteran: a former soldier

Additional Reading

Brumbaugh, Gaius, Marcus. *"Revolutionary War Records, Volume 1, Virginia"*. Washington D.C., Gaius Marcus Brumbaugh, 1936.

Bell, Carol Willsey. *"Ohio-Lands: Steubenville Land Office 1800-1820"*. Youngstown: Carol Willsey Bell, 1985.

Bell, Carol Willsey. *"Ohio-Guide to Genealogical Sources"*. Baltimore: Genealogical Publishing Co., Inc. 1988.

Berry, Ellen T. and David A. *"Early Ohio Settlers - Purchasers of Land in Southeastern Ohio, 1800-1840"*. (Marietta Land Office), Baltimore: Genealogical Publishing Co., 1984.

Berry, Ellen T. and David A. *"Early Ohio Settlers - Purchasers of Land in Southwestern Ohio, 1800-1840"*. (Cincinnati Land Office), Baltimore: Genealogical Publishing Co., 1986.

Berry, Ellen T. and David A. *"Early Ohio Settlers - Purchasers of Land in East and East Central Ohio, 1800-1840"*. Baltimore: Genealogical Publishing Co., 1989.

Carstensen, Vernon, ed. *"The Public Lands: Studies in the History of the Public Domain"*. Madison, 1963.

Clark, Marie Taylor. *"Ohio Lands: Chillicothe Land Office, 1800-1829"*. Chillicothe: Marie Taylor Clark, 1984.

Clark, Marie Taylor. *"Ohio Lands: South of the Indian Boundary Line"*. Chillicothe: Marie Taylor Clark, 1984.

Downs, Randolph C. *"Evolution of Ohio County Boundaries"*. Ohio Archaeological and Historical Publications No. XXXVI, Columbus: OA&H Society, 1927. Reprinted 1970.

Dyer, Albion Morris. *"First Ownership of Ohio Lands"*. Baltimore: Genealogical Publishing Co., Inc. 1911. Reprinted 1982.

Gates, Paul W. *"History of Public Land Law Development"*. Washington D.C.: Public Land Law Review Commission, 1968.

Hulbert, Archer B., ed. *"Ohio in the Time of the Confederation"*. 2 Vols. Marietta: Marietta College, 1917.

Hulbert, Archer B. *"The Records of the Original Proceedings of the Ohio Company"*. 2 Vols. Marietta: Marietta College, 1917.

Peters, William E. *"Ohio Lands and Their History"*. 3rd Ed., Athens: W.E. Peters, 1930. Reprinted.

Riegel, Mayburt Stephenson. *"Early Ohioans' Residences from the Land Grant Records"*. Mansfield: Ohio Genealogical Society, 1976.

Rohrbough, Malcom J. *"The Land Office Business"*. New York: Oxford University Press, 1968.

Treat, Payson, J. *"The National Land System 1785-1820"*. New York, 1910.

Sherman, Christopher E. *"Original Land Subdivisions"*. Volume III, Final Report - Ohio Topographic Survey. Columbus: Ohio Department of Natural Resources, 1925. Reprinted 1982. Wall Map separate.

Smith, Clifford Neal. *"Federal Land Series, Volumes 1-4"*. Chicago: American Library Association, 1972-1987.

Smith, Alma Aicholtz. *"The Virginia Military Surveys of Clermont and Hamilton Counties, Ohio 1787-1849"*. Cincinnati: Alma Aicholtz Smith, 1985.

White, C. Albert. *"A History of the Rectangular Survey System"*. Washington D.C.: Government Printing Office, 1982.

We gratefully acknowledge the following people and organizations for providing *Along the Ohio Trail* with images and information:

Dr. George W. Knepper, Distinguished Professor of History, Emeritus, The University of Akron for editorial guidance.

The Ohio Historical Society for use of most of the images in this book that were provided by the Archives/Library Division.

The University of Cincinnati for permission to print the illustrations of Fort Ancient, Stubbs Woodhenge and the Hopewell site.

The Ohio Department of Natural Resources for the use of illustrations from C.E. Sherman's "Original Land Subdivisions."

To the many researchers who provided advice and suggestions for this publication, sincere thanks and grateful appreciation for all your help.

The book would not have been possible without the help of many employees in various departments of the Auditor of State's Office. We would like to give special thanks to:

R. Dennis Gilbert, Director of Graphics

Jeff Roberts, Asst. Director of Graphics